VENTURE FORWARD

VENTURE FORWARD

LESSONS FROM LEADERS

JASON KRAUS

NEW DEGREE PRESS

VENTURE FORWARD

Lessons from Leaders

ISBN   978-1-64137-290-9   *Paperback*

              978-1-64137-475-0   *Ebook*

This book is dedicated to Nina Vlasic, for cheering me on though the writer's block and always pushing me to Venture Forward to reach my goals.

CONTENTS

SPECIAL ACKNOWLEDGEMENT

———

I'd to thank my Mom and Dad, my brother Adam, and my girlfriend Nina for the constant support and motivation throughout my journey. I'd like to thank all of my friends, family and the local Boston startup community for sharing, promoting and cheering me on, I couldn't have done it without all of you. I'd like to give a big thank you to the Creator Institute and New Degree Press, especially Erik Koester and Brian Bies for leading me through the publishing process and turning this book into a reality.

In creating this book, I had the fortune of connecting with and interviewing an incredible selections of leaders, startup founders and CEOs, that helped me piece together the stories and lessons that I proudly present to you today. These are the individuals and chosen leaders you will hear from throughout the book:

Laurel Taylor, CEO of FutureFuel.io (http://futurefuel.io/)
Henrique DuBrugras, CEO of Brex
John Lohavichan, Co-Founder of Mattervest and Founder of TrustFuss
Marissa Sergi, Founder of RedHead Wines
Atisha Patel, Co-Founder of NotiCare
Deepak Atyam, CEO of Tri-D Dynamics
Trey Bowles, Chairman of the Dallas Entrepreneurship Center
Kyle Herron, CEO of Seio and co-founder of Frontier Mining
Samantha Zirkin, CEO of Point93
Adam Sobol, CEO of CareBand

Thank you to everyone involved who made these interviews possible. Additionally you will hear stories from secondary interviews and leaders throughout this book as well, and I would like to extend a thank you to the leaders themselves, as well as the media, podcast hosts, journalists, and event organizers who helped share their stories that I have the fortune of passing on to you. I'd like to thank all of the supporters who preordered a copy of my book and helped me kick off the publication, you are all featured in the acknowledgments section at the end of this book.

INTRODUCTION

———

"It was like night and day," said Kate Dwyer, co-founder of eCommerce marketplace Witchsy. "It would take me days to get a response, but Keith could not only get a response and a status update, but also be asked if he wanted anything else or if there was anything else that Keith needed help with."

Kate and her co-founder Penelope faced hurdles as female founders when they launched their marketplace. Developers and partners would be slow to respond and use phrases like, "Okay, girls…" in addressing their emails.

They were not being taken seriously.

So what did they do?

They created a fake third co-founder named Keith Mann to email under, and the difference was incredible—lightning-fast responses and turnaround times! Keith was looked up to and admired as the fake male co-founder while Kate and Penelope were seen as doing a "cute project.[1]"

We all root for Kate and Penelope.

Their story may seem to be one of those "triumphant female founders showcase inherent sexism and find a way to beat the system." But it led me to dig deeper into the problem and explore something entirely different: *Do today's founders really need to "look the part" in order to raise money?*

**

I didn't grow up thinking about business or being an entrepreneur. I dreamed of playing shortstop for the Red Sox, becoming an astronaut, or an author—well, one of these is coming true!

I always loved games. Growing up playing Monopoly and UNO with friends and family, I loved new games and loved to read but hated reading instructions. The thrill was in

---

1   John Paul Titlow. 2017. "These Women Entrepreneurs Created A Fake Male Cofounder To Dodge Startup Sexism." Fast Company. Fast Company. August 29, 2017.

figuring out how to play the game, making up my own rules if I needed to. Although I never packaged the UNO revision I came up with and tried to sell it to Mattel (they later came out with a similar version of the game and called it DOS), the spirit of curiosity and creativity in a quest to make things more exciting always stuck with me.

The Night Owl App, my first official startup, developed in my senior year at Colgate University, became the biggest learning experience any college student could ask for. I learned how to go to through the ideation phase as my roommates and I wished there was a way to check out the bar scene downtown before venturing into the frigid upstate New York winter. I found freelance developers overseas to join my project and help me develop my app and began spreading the word and gathering feedback around campus for my vision. However, my research could have been stronger before launch. A few months after publishing the app, I received a cease and desist letter from two separate entities with Mobile Applications named Night Owl, one of which sent a complaint through the iOS App Store.

I would take the lessons I had learned and build on them at Babson College's Master of Science in Entrepreneurial Leadership program. In the first few months at Babson, I found the perfect combination of my love of finance and the excitement of entrepreneurship while interning with the Boston

Harbor Angels group, which held its monthly meetings at the school. Helping set up the meetings and taking meeting notes to send out to the group, I learned the ins and outs of what the investors were looking for in each of the deals that came through and gained a passion for the world of angel and VC investing.

After several months of serial networking with every alumni, personal, or LinkedIn connection in the venture capital space I could make, I landed a position as an associate in the venture arm of a local family office in May 2015. I quickly learned the ropes of further evaluating deal flow, as well as the internal marketing of the venture capital fund itself.

In March of 2016, as the firm built toward raising a new fund, I began picking up some freelance advisory work on the side, taking what I had learned in my investment roles to help early-stage startups create pitch decks, financials, business plans, and more. By May of 2016, I created a website and brand, launched Prepare 4 VC, and began to pursue my business full time under the mission of helping startups raise capital from an investor's perspective.

Since the launch, I have worked with B2B technology, healthcare, fashion, aerospace, social media, eCommerce, FinTech companies, and more, building up a brand and extending my network of partners and connections in the space to add additional value to the companies we work with. I've joined several startups in larger roles over the last few years and have transitioned back to the investment side as well. I co-founded an alternative investment group Equity Venture Partners, which focuses on connecting investors with our deal flow of early-stage startups and co-investment opportunities in commercial real estate, and became a venture partner on a micro-VC fund, EQx Fund, which focuses on investing in emotional capital through startups with incredible leadership teams.

Now, I have distilled all my experience into the key mission of *Venture Forward* —inspiring and enabling innovation in the world around me. I have intertwined my personal experiences with interviews and research on an amazing group of entrepreneurs that will inspire and guide you in the next phase of your entrepreneurial adventure.

Although 99.99 percent of companies don't look like Facebook or Apple, we all picture these firms as the icons of the ideal startup while aspiring to be the next Mark Zuckerberg or Steve Jobs.

Is dropping out of college to start a company *really* the way to go as an entrepreneur?

**

Most companies are built on the backbone of strong education and experience. Despite popular startup books and media hype, 95 percent of startup entrepreneurs have at least a Bachelor's degree and the average age for startup founders is 40.[2]

Who are the fastest-growing group of entrepreneurs? Since 1997, the number of businesses owned by African-American women has more than tripled, making them the fastest-growing group of business owners in the US. Overall, female business ownership has increased by 74 percent since 1997[3].

And while we hear success stories of serial successful entrepreneurs like the "PayPal Mafia," which included Elon Musk (Tesla), Peter Thiel (YCombinator), Reid Hoffman (LinkedIn) and several others, any startup experience (even failures) can lead to future success. To this end, a study has shown that startup founders who have failed in the past are more likely to succeed in their next venture than the average first-time entrepreneur. Founders of a previously successful business have a 30 percent chance of success with their next venture, while founders who have failed at a prior business have a 20 percent chance of succeeding versus an 18 percent

---

2   "36 Fascinating Facts About Startups." 2018. Factinate. December 12, 2018.

3   Kouloupoulos, Thomas. 2015. "5 of the Most Surprising Statistics About Startups." Inc.Com. Inc. October 21, 2015.

chance of success for first-time entrepreneurs. Learning from the successes and failures of previous ventures along the way can make a significant difference in future ventures[4].

Most people may not find the idea of spending several years creating a failing business so the next venture has a better shot of success appealing. Instead, most would agree that they would rather leverage the lessons of other founders and other ventures that have succeeded to achieve their own success. This has become the crux of the mission behind *Venture Forward: Lessons from Leaders.*

Do you check all the boxes on our startup checklist?

- Male team
- White founders
- A business founder and a technical founder
- Located in San Francisco/Silicon Valley
- Working to raise huge venture capital rounds
- In a trendy market (blockchain. Ai, virtual reality, etc.)

There is this "one-size fits all" mentality on how to build and scale a successful startup. In reality, startups come in many shapes and sizes built from an eclectic group of individuals. Instead of the typical approach of road-mapping

---

4   Koulopoulos, Thomas. 2015. "5 of the Most Surprising Statistics About Startups." Inc.Com. Inc. October 21, 2015.

your company's creation, the best approach to the startup process is asking yourself, "At this stage in my business, what have other entrepreneurs done that has succeeded and what mistakes did they make?"

This book is a collection of lessons and stories that can shape your vision and strategy, giving you the tools to choose what makes sense for leading your own venture forward.

And in fact, I'll show you that it is more important to focus on highlighting your own unique checklist rather than trying to fit yourself into some theoretical perfect startup model.

You don't need to create your own Keith to raise money.

You just need to be you.

**

Work your way through the entrepreneurship section of Barnes and Noble and you will see that all of the business advice assumes you look like, or want to be, the next Facebook or Google.

And perhaps just as importantly, they assume you likely look like Mark Zuckerberg or Steve Jobs or the aforementioned Keith.

But what happens when you don't?

Are you a female founder tired of trying to be taken seriously?

In this book, you will learn how Laurel Taylor, the founder of FinTech platform FutureFuel, launched and built up a startup that signed major customers onto her platform and just raised an $11 million series A round. She is a female entrepreneur who *ventured forward.*

Are you an immigrant founder struggling with adapting your business in the US?

In this book, you will learn from Henrique Dubugras, founder of Brex, the first corporate credit card for startups. As an immigrant entrepreneur, he could not secure personal lines of credit to grow the company, and even though he had $120,000 in the bank from YCombinator, he could not get a corporate credit card. Instead of settling for the status quo, he embraced the opportunity to make a difference and launched the first credit for startups, *venturing forward* to the Unicorn Club with a $1 billion+ startup.

Are you a solo founder or non-technical founder?

Marisa Sergi started RedHead Wines as a solo founder, entering her modern and enticing wine labels into business plan competitions in college. She won every competition she entered and has built a business through partnerships and distributors to land top clients and press as she builds the RedHead Wine Brand. She found the strength to *venture forward* as a solo founder to build a powerful brand in the competitive wine industry.

Are you from a city or town outside of the typical startup hubs?

Trey Bowles is a serial entrepreneur who has made it his mission to create startup hubs in Dallas, Texas and six smaller cities around the area. He founded The Dallas Entrepreneurship Center to bring expert mentors who could share their expertise with entrepreneurs to give them a leg up by learning from the successes and failures of those who have done it before. Trey has helped his community *venture forward* to a $130 million economic impact in the Greater Dallas areas.

Are you focused on bootstrapping your business through cash flows?

Atisha Patel, the founder of Noticare, a hospital-to-parent communication platform for the ICU, focused her efforts on bootstrapping her company forward to growth. She leveraged her full-time role to supplement her income as she started the company, leveraging a variety of resources including an eager computer science class at Drexel University to bootstrap and launch her brand to revenues. She has taken on Noticare full-time with a powerful team behind her and runs a boot camp for high school students to learn from her techniques in taking their *ventures forward.*

Does your market ignore the trends and buzzwords that are making waves?

Joe Gebbia of Airbnb shares his story of creating a new business in the bed in breakfast space, which was far from a trendy industry at the time. His experience hosting a stranger on an air mattress fostered the original idea, fueled by a rental experience to make quick cash for rent with his roommate and now co-founder that led to the brand. The tip that helped them *venture forward* to unicorn status: "It's okay to do things early on that don't scale."—Paul Graham of YCombinator

**

Most people think there is one startup trajectory to take, but if you've never started a company, joined a startup, had a lemonade stand, or even sold a Beanie Baby on eBay, you may still be an entrepreneur at heart.

This book is designed to help entrepreneurs across the country reach their goals by learning from entrepreneurs who do not fit the stereotypical startup mold. There are no identical pathways toward success but rather a collection of building blocks we can all implement on our paths when the opportunity fits.

Who this book is NOT for:

- You dropped out of Stanford because your company was just growing too fast to do both.
- You were a lead developer at Google, and you already have offers to purchase the patent on your incredible software on day one.
- You have all the capital you need and investors lined up from your last few exits and an audience waiting for your product release.

This is for the 99 percent of founders who don't look like that… but 99 percent of the advice out there targets the select group above.

LET'S VENTURE FORWARD…

THE EUREKA MOMENT

"Your best ideas, those eureka moments that turn the world upside down, seldom come when you're juggling emails, rushing to meet the 5 P.M. deadline, or straining to make your voice heard in a high-stress meeting. They come when you're walking the dog, soaking in the bath, or swinging in a hammock."

—CARL HONORE

"Why couldn't we get a credit card?"

Henrique DuBugras and Pedro Franchesci were successful entrepreneurs and enrolled in the world-renowned YCombinator, an accelerator program that brings together many of the top up-and-coming startups in the world under one roof for three months of training, support, and resources to gear companies for their demo-day pitch to a packed auditorium of 1000 eager investors. They had previously built and sold Brazil's leading payment processing platform Pagar.me while in high school and were back together in Silicon Valley, building their vision for a virtual reality company.

And yet, they had a problem that even they couldn't fathom in today's world with their pedigree and connections.

"We couldn't get a corporate credit card—none of our YCombinator batchmates could either," Henrique DuBugras said. "It was crazy. We all had $120,000 in the bank."

Some of their peer startup founders opted to run company expenses through their personal credit cards; however, Henrique and Pedro were from Brazil with no American credit history and limited options.

They could have gotten frustrated, walked away from the problem, or just moved on to something else. But they didn't and instead, something magical happened.

Eureka.

They took this business roadblock and turned it into an opportunity to disrupt an outdated system.

And that's the secret advantage most founders don't realize they need.

FINDING PURE GOLD

One of the key drivers of innovation and startup ideas is a "pain point." While others strive to avoid problems or painful situations, entrepreneurs view them as opportunities to build a company around, with a captive audience that needs their pain relieved.

Successful businesses differentiate from the competition by demonstrating a market need for their solution. Find a problem no other company has solved and you have the crux of your idea. Figure out the solution and you have the beginning of your startup.

This is known as *product market fit.*

In fact, according to a 2018 CBinsights poll, the top reason for startup failure is a lack of market need[5]. The entrepreneurs who face those eureka moments and solve problems no one else can go on to build the startups we all know and love.

---

5   "The Top 20 Reasons Startups Fail." 2019. CB Insights Research. March 15, 2019.

Gary "Vee" Vaynerchuck, serial successful entrepreneur and investor, received constant rejections on many of his ideas, getting shot down dozens of times before becoming the successful entrepreneur turned investor and startup influencer he is today. This excerpt from his blog serves a powerful lesson on pursuing ideas with our strengths to build great companies:

> "I think I was wired backwards somewhere along the road, because I actually prefer that everybody think I'm wrong. Is that weird?
>
> When somebody tries to tell me something won't work, or rejects an idea, it only makes me want to pursue it more.
>
> I've dealt with some pretty harsh rejection in my career. And when I say rejection, I really mean it big-time. People have mocked entire businesses I believed in. When I launched WineLibrary.com, people laughed at e-commerce. When I started my agency Vayner Media, the overall sentiment in 2009 was that an agency devoted to social would never take off.
>
> So yes: rejection happens. To everyone. A lot. But the truth is, I don't give a crap what anyone says. And

this is a mindset that I believe many many people can benefit from.

If you're in any part of the world of business, rejection is just something you are going to run into. It's inevitable. People will want to challenge you and question your ideas, and you should welcome that. It is absolutely necessary in helping you to figure out exactly how much you want something and why.

But when you feel something in your gut, you can't ignore it.

So what do you do with all that negativity?

You turn it into positivity. Rise to the challenge. Accept that the climb might be the best part of this whole thing. Because once you're at the top, that's it. You're just there. But when you're on your way up, that's where the real hard work comes in. And when you're a business person, that hard work feels really good, right?

Make it a point to prove people wrong. Get excited about showing people how right you are. Dealing with rejection means facing it head on, proving it's not true, then on to the next one.

So yeah. Maybe this kind of thinking is a bit backwards. I'm a big fan of betting on strengths and ignoring the competition. But it feels so good to show people you were right, and I would hate for you all to miss out on that.

*I would hate even more for one of you to miss out on an enormous opportunity because you let someone bring you down. **This is me telling you right now: prove them wrong. You can do this. Now hustle.**"*

Entrepreneurship is a state of mind. It involves taking risks and chasing opportunities where others do not see the same vision. It involves viewing problems as opportunities and solutions as potential companies. Companies you can grow and scale to bring the vision to life. Entrepreneurship, innovation, and invention have been around for centuries, turning the craziest of ideas into reality.

**

In the 3rd century B.C., the famous Greek Mathematician Archimedes was faced with a daunting task that future founders face every day: a problem to solve with no clear solution using the technology of the time. In this case, the newly minted King of Syracuse in Sicily, King Hiero II, needed a new crown. The king hired a goldsmith and gave him one of his bars of gold to use to create the crown. The goldsmith delivered a crown to the king, but the king suspected that the goldsmith had cheated him. It was a common scam at the time to mix cheaper metals into the gold and keep some of the remaining gold as a profit, but the king had no way of proving the authenticity of the crown.

There was no science or technological method at the time to test the king's theory. The king hired Archimedes with the challenge of proving whether the crown was made from pure gold without damaging it.

Archimedes spent countless hours contemplating and hypothesizing, studying the works of fellow mathematicians and scientists, and testing different methods with no results. He finally took a break to decompress, filling up a bath to relax.

"When I got into the tub," Archimedes reasoned, "my body displaced water. Now, there must be a relationship between my volume and the volume of water my body displaced—because if I weren't so big, less water would have spilled on my floor."

He jumped out of the bathtub exclaiming, "Eureka!" (I have found it!) as he ran down the stairs, out the door, and across town—still fully naked—to the king in the castle. He would be able to prove once and for all if the crown was pure gold!

He knew silver was less dense than gold, and his discovery of water displacement, later known as the Archimedes Principle, would allow him to figure out if the density of the crown matched that of gold. The king's hiring of Archimedes and his discovery led to an entrepreneurial solution and a legacy that still lives on today[6].

**

You may have already had the eureka moment that launched you into innovation (with or without the streaking part), or it may be yet to come.

Innovation and that "AHA!" moment come in all shapes and sizes.

A STARTUP IS BORN

Henrique DuBugras and Pedro Franchesci had the entrepreneurial spirit running through their veins from an early age. At the age of 12, they connected in Brazil through playing online video games. Henrique wanted video game skins and characters that were expensive and his family could not afford them at the time. Instead of giving up or finding boring side jobs to earn some cash, Henrique went straight to the

---

6   "About Eureka!" 2019. Bellarmine.Edu. 2019.

problem and started looking for developers to code and sell video game skins and other add-ons to enhance his gaming experience. He reached out to the gaming community on Twitter and got connected to Pedro, who claimed to know how to develop everything Henrique needed.

"He sent me over some of his work, and I was amazed by what he had done, but then I asked how old he was, and he told me he was 12, as well," Henrique described. "I didn't believe him and heard stories in school of older people trying to pretend to be teenagers to connect with them. After all, what 12-year old could code like that? It wasn't until almost two years later that we finally reconnected, and I realized Pedro really was the same age as me and incredibly skilled at development. We've worked on every single startup together since."

Henrique and Pedro developed several startups and were winning local business plan competitions. As they worked on one video game accessory platform, they realized they needed a payment processing application to plug into the system they had developed. They explored all of their options with the existing platforms on the marketplace and each one had a shortcoming in the feature set, price, or integrations. So, they decided to develop their own payment processing platform.

As they proceeded, user feedback on their skins and platform were gaining some momentum but the feature people were most excited about was their novel payment processing technology. It was incredibly efficient and user-friendly compared to other systems being offered in Brazil at the time, and they started getting requests to take on payment projects for other companies.

The duo soon took their efforts to this aspect full-time and the new platform Pagar.me, which means "Pay Me" in Portuguese, soon became a huge success. Known as the "PayPal of Brazil," it became one of the most developer-friendly payment processing platforms. Henrique and Pedro, who were only in high school at the time, sold Pagar.me to pursue degrees at Stanford University and head to the San Francisco area to break into the US startup scene for their next ventures.

They began working on a virtual reality startup and were quickly accepted in the prestigious accelerator YCombinator (YC). Upon receiving the $120,000 investment that comes along with acceptance to YC, Henrique and Pedro dropped out of school to pursue the opportunity full-time. Yet they still faced roadblocks from traditional banking institutions. The founders scrapped their original startup idea and created Brex to address the startup financing problems of founders like themselves.

Brex set a mission and new metric for startups, using equity financing in the startup's bank account as the main source of approval for their corporate credit card. And with this idea, they could leverage their payment expertise to make a huge splash in the market[7].

"When we sold our last company in payments, we agreed we were done with payments; dealing with banks and regulation seemed so hard. So, we wanted to do something different. Virtual Reality (VR) seemed like the fleeting edge of technology, so we said, 'Let's do a VR startup.' We got into YC with our idea, but soon we realized we had no clue what we were doing. We realized what we love is financial services and what we are as founders are mostly prepared to do, right? We had an unfair advantage in building Brex because we had built a payments company before, and we had an unfair disadvantage building VR because we know nothing about hardware companies or VR per se," Henrique explained in an interview[8].

Brex is on a powerful mission to use the team's expertise in FinTech to create a world where no companies face the barriers to startup credit that Henrique and Pedro had faced. And the mission is off to an incredible start. I had originally

---

7   Wieczner, Jen. 2018. "Y Combinator's Favorite Credit Card Just Raised $50 Million from PayPal Founders." Fortune. Fortune. June 19, 2018.
8   "IVP's Hyper-Growth Podcast: The Hyper-Growth of Brex with Co-Founder and CEO, Henrique Dubugras - IVP." 2019. IVP. September 9, 2019.

connected with Henrique and Brex as the Chapter Director for Boston's Startup Grind. Fascinated by the Pagar.me story, further conversations with Henrique confirmed the power of what they were building with Brex, and we lined up an event for September 2018. Unfortunately, a few days prior to the event, Henrique's team informed me that he was caught up in an urgent matter on the West Coast and could not attend our event, hinting I would shortly find out in a press release. I hoped the magnitude of the announcement would overcome my disappointment at having to cancel our event.

Sure enough, I received an email with the press release noting how Henrique and the team had just secured a $125 million financing round at a $1 billion+ valuation, becoming the youngest entrepreneurs in the Unicorn Club (the nickname for achieving a fantastical figure of a $1 billion company) at age 22.

I think that qualifies as pretty huge news.

Since then, I've had the opportunity to see Henrique pitch at the Forbes 30 Under 30 Conference in Boston, Pedro present at the StartupGrind Global event in Silicon Valley, and Larissa Rocha, the first hire, lead a round-table at the NextGen Conference. The story gets more amazing every time.

**

Entrepreneurs are not normal. By definition, "an entrepreneur is a person who organizes and operates a business or businesses, taking on *greater than normal* financial risks in order to do so[9]." Where do entrepreneurs stand out from the crowd, and how can you embrace your own eureka moments?

Scenario 1: Mary is a graphic artist who loves to express her work visually and build brands. She took a stable job two years ago to run social media marketing efforts at a late-stage startup. She enjoys her content creation pieces but hates the majority of her work, which revolves around data entry, analytics, and mundane tasks of copying and pasting different posts to each channel and moderating the users. What does Mary do about it?

The "normal" response: Do nothing; stick it out. After all, only 45 percent of Americans actually like their jobs so at least Mary is ahead with liking part of her job[10]. Work is work for a reason; it's not supposed to be enjoyable. And plus, Mary and her friends meet up after work every Thursday night at The Watering Hole to talk about the terrible week at work over gin and tonics.

---

9   "Entrepreneur Definition - Google Search." 2019. Google.Com. 2019.
10 G.E. Miller. 2019. "I Hate My Job! 55% of Americans Agree. 5 Steps to Fix It." 20somethingfinance.Com. August 25, 2019.

But Mary isn't normal; she is an entrepreneur. She joins forums and communities of other social media marketers and finds that others share the same frustrations. Where her colleagues see this as just part of the job, Mary wonders, *What if there was a way to automate all of the boring tasks so that we can get back to creating content?* While others just dream of solutions to their everyday problems in work and life, Mary is an entrepreneur and takes action. She develops a vision, continues interviewing others in her position, and connects with an old friend who works as a developer and is eager to come on board. Before she knows it, Mary has a startup and jumps in with both feet to take the *venture forward*.

Scenario 2: Frank is a diehard New England Patriots fan, has season tickets, and goes to every home game the team has. One day after looking up Tom Brady's statistics from the last game, he "randomly" sees a Facebook advertisement about custom T-shirts with a goat on the front and G.O.A.T (Greatest of All Time AKA Tom Brady) on the back. He buys one to wear to the next game, and everyone around him loves it and asks where they can get one.

The **normal** response would be to take the compliment in stride and give everyone the website link to order their own. But Frank has a eureka moment and sees a new opportunity. He marks down the sizes of everyone interested on his phone, and after the game, bulk orders 100 shirts for the next week. He gets to the parking lot early next time, sells the shirts at a premium, and makes an instant profit, selling out by the first quarter.

Eureka moments can come in any shape or size and at any moment. Entrepreneurs recognize these moments and seize the opportunity to take a risk and make something happen. As we will learn later on, startups can change and pivot and scale along the way with a variety of pathways, but they all start from a vision and a belief that the entrepreneur can build something new that will make a difference in their lives and the lives of those around them.

FINDING MY OWN EUREKA

My eureka moment leading to Prepare 4 VC in February 2016 came from statistics gathered while working in the venture capital and angel investment space. Those statistics were staggering:

- Between 60-100 pitch decks were reviewed each month,
- Only a handful of companies move on to formal meetings and pitches in a highly competitive vetting process.
- There is an industry average of only 1.5 percent of startups getting funded.

- With a knowledge of the investment side and knowing what differentiated startups that made it past the initial screening from the rest, I knew their amazing businesses and backgrounds did not shine through in their pitch decks.

I put my expertise to work in helping startups raise capital from the investor's perspective. Within two weeks of the initial idea, I bought the www.Prepare4VC.com domain and launched a drag-and-drop website through Sitebuilder.com to showcase my new brand. I reached out to a handful of entrepreneurs through LinkedIn and applied for freelance projects on UpWork and HourlyNerd for pitch deck design, financial projections, and more. At first, my rates were discounted with the focus on proving if the business model was something startups would pay for. By doing this, I was able to collect enough samples, feedback, and stories from founders to shape the company into what it is today.

It all started from an idea I was willing to quickly jump on and iterate based on feedback.

**

"There's an app for that!" The phrase Apple trademarked and made famous in their iPhone 3G commercial in 2009 has grown to be even truer today[11]. The Apple store now has over 1.8 million applications in every industry you can think of, offering everything from transportation, productivity, games, and live streaming right from our phones and tablets[12]. Our first instinct in today's ecosystem can be to build an app or software application to solve all our problems. They are increasingly easier to build, test out and get to market. Build a website and throw it on the app store and users will come, right?

With so many applications and technology-based businesses, it is getting increasingly difficult to compete for users' attention and downloads. Startups are increasingly leveraging technology while building a moat through other aspects of their business. Take a look at the startups below with easily replicated technology that were able to differentiate themselves with unique competitive advantages:

Facebook: The technology to find and connect online to share messages and write on walls already existed on sites like MySpace, Friendster, and other social media platforms. *Eureka Moment:* People wanted to connect with networks they trusted. Facebook launched with verified university emails

---

11 "Apple Trademarks 'There's an App for That' - CNN.Com." 2010. Cnn.Com. 2010.

12 "App Stores: Number of Apps in Leading App Stores 2018 | Statista." 2018. Statista. Statista. 2018.

before expanding, with the vision of scaling so that if everyone's closest friends were on the Facebook platform, switching to a new platform would be incredibly difficult.

Wayfair: ECommerce technology and applications had existed in every business including furniture. *Eureka Moment:* Founders Steve Conine and Niraj Shah had a vision that if they analyzed well-performing and trending products to launch them on an eCommerce channel, they could create a high-margin, profitable furniture marketplace by leveraging technology[13].

Dollar Shave Club: The company was not the first to develop subscription boxes and was not founded on the hopes of providing the best or even the cheapest razor blades on the market. *Eureka Moment:* The "club" part of Dollar Shave Club would be the key ingredient to success. CEO Michael Dubin created the legendary launch video for the service in March 2012, which has 26 million hits on YouTube to date and led to 12,000 orders in the first two days, crashing the site. He appealed to the audience and gave viewers a sense of belonging and a community of fellow shavers was born.

While these are famous startup examples that can be deemed successful, one driver of the lessons in this book is that startups can be successful in all shapes and sizes by following the

---

13   "Wayfair." 2019a. Wayfair. 2019.

path and lessons that are best for their business. There is no one-size-fits-all model.

If your vision leverages large network effects and exposure like Facebook, you may need large venture capital financing and marketing budgets to achieve success, while in other types of companies, bootstrapping makes the most sense. You can launch a successful local craft beer, consulting business, or fashion accessory as a profitable cash flow business with limited or no outside investment. Some companies are started by leveraging existing technology in new ways, while others, especially in the healthcare/life-sciences and Ai/Deep Technology, rely heavily on research & development to create proprietary intellectual property.

**

As an entrepreneur or someone who dreams of being an entrepreneur, it is important to always be on the lookout for new ideas. While most people wait for applications and products they can buy to enhance their lives, entrepreneurs look for the opportunities that need enhancing and create a solution around them.

What will be your eureka moment?

"There's this famous observation that I totally believe: Great startup ideas are the ones that lie in the intersection of the Venn diagram of 'is a good idea' and 'looks like a bad idea.' So you want most people to think it's a bad idea and thus not compete with you until you get giant. But for it to secretly be good." —Sam Altman, Chairman of YCombinator

- The best ideas can come at any moment.
- Entrepreneurs run toward challenges and pain points as business opportunities, while others see them as obstacles.
- The eureka moment and differentiation can come in many shapes: the idea itself, novel technology, marketing strategy, community it supports location, etc. The key is to align the company goals with the strategy you will use to get there.

FIND YOUR PROBLEM

———

"If we tried to think of a good idea, we wouldn't have been able to think of a good idea. You just have to find the solution for a problem in your own life."

—BRIAN CHESKY, CO-FOUNDER OF AIRBNB

"I had the idea for Uber almost twenty years ago…"

Sure, okay.

But you're not a billionaire, so what happened?

We have all seen that there are good ideas for startups.

I also believe that there are no truly bad ideas for startups.

That said, there *are* certainly bad startups: bad leadership, product-market fit, corporate structure, market timing, execution, and a variety of other factors.

But the ideas themselves are usually within the same ballpark as another venture that will become hugely successful.

And many of the famous startups we know and love today were not anything that seemed like "brilliant ideas" at the time.

Remember, before Uber, when we were told as kids to never get in a car with a stranger? Did it really seem like a good idea to replace trusted taxi drivers with random strangers as drivers? And yet, here we are with a $100 billion company predicated on a questionable idea with a strong team and great execution.

INNOVATING FROM PERSONAL NEED

Nine percent interest.

When Laurel Taylor was accepted to the Massachusetts Institute of Technology (MIT) Sloan MBA program, she decided to look into student loans for her tuition. She had a solid work history and a perfect credit score, having paid off her student loans, and a job lined up as the head of industry for a business unit of Google.

Yet, from all of the options she found, the best terms she was able to obtain was a nine percent annual interest rate.

Nine percent.

That personal problem would change the entire face of her entrepreneurial career.

**

"I have been a closeted entrepreneur my whole life but also in corporate. Before I founded FutureFuel, I led a global business unit for Google. Google is very much about inspiring entrepreneurial behavior and the bias to action but really Google is a brand that we all know," Laurel said, explaining her path into entrepreneurship as I interviewed her on a StartupGrind Boston Fireside Chat.

Like most American college graduates, FutureFuel Founder and CEO Laurel Taylor faced what seemed like an insurmountable amount of student debt.

"I think we've surrendered to the fact that 70 percent of us graduate with a student loan debt," Laurel explained. "I think all I did was accept this and I was living, not really questioning it until I went back to school at MIT. I kind of naively thought, 'All right, well, I've got a credit score over

800, I have a job, let me see what this would look like. Would it make more sense to take out student loans? I was given a nine percent interest rate, and I'm not talking about sinful credit. I had a lot of work history, never defaulted, and again, my credit score was perfect, so that was a really profound moment for me. If I'm getting a nine percent interest rate, well, what is everybody else getting?"

Nine percent interest?! With a perfect credit score, a job at Google, and an MBA program at MIT!

With further research, Laurel found that the issue has become such a crisis that 40 percent of millennial employees with student debt are forced to opt-out of traditional 401K benefits because they need to allocate the capital to debt repayment and living expenses. The wheels started to turn, and Laurel dug in deeper on the second problem of opting out of benefits[14].

"I was at Google, which was absolutely an honor to be part of Google and to have the opportunity to lead a global business unit for them. I also realized that the top 20 tech brands have an average of 15 months retention, so whether you're Google or Facebook, you have under two years. So if the top 20 tech brands cannot hold on to employees for longer than

---

14 Taylor, Laurel. 2018. "Laurel Taylor (FutureFuel.Io)- Building and Scaling a Mission-Driven Startup." YouTube. August 2, 2018.

15 months, what does that mean for everyone else? And to me, it was all just very intuitive that student debt-centric benefits would be the way to really drive what we call love and loyalty: You've got my back, so I'm going to have yours."

Laurel had her eureka moment, where the pieces of the puzzle were starting to come together. But it was still just a theory. She reached out to every employer she could to gather feedback and test the market response before bringing her vision to life.

"I started pitching employers, and I started hearing from employers I would meet with: They would tell me for 45 minutes about just how massive these issues were. *How do I acquire top talent? How do I retain talent? How do I compete and not get my ass kicked by Google and everybody else? How do I solve this problem? Here all the problems that we have, we're looking for ways, we have all these perks and nothing's really working, so yes, I'm willing to try it and your ROI is that if I offer repayment and they stay with me two months longer I break even, and if they stay a year, I can fund the benefit for 14 other people.*"

Boston FinTech startup FutureFuel, a winner of the Financial Solutions 2018 $250,000 innovation challenge, the South By Southwest FinTech startup competition ($4,000 prize), and a portfolio company of Boston Harbor Angels and the EQx

Fund, was founded to solve a pain point the founder faced that affects millions of Americans every day[15].

"Prior to Google, I worked for many brands that were not known, and I started my career dialing for dollars. I made 75 dials a day in my first job out of college, and I drove revenue essentially for several different organizations over a 15-year horizon from small companies, making them big. So I always lived as an intrapreneur but for me when I was going through a couple of different life-changing events that happened around the time that I founded FutureFuel, I just felt like that was really my path and purpose, so it was time for me to get on with it and actually get it done."

For Laurel, entrepreneurship and the ability to innovate in her everyday work was a key element in the roles she pursued, but it took a real passion of her own to drive her to start her own company in FutureFuel. The mission of the company is not just to ease financial hardship but rather to "Crush Student Debt." Starting from a simple problem that has plagued others across the United States for decades, Laurel was able to address the issue at hand by creating a new company. As I write this chapter, her company continues to take off with

---

15   Ziad Moukheiber. 2018a. "SXSW Announces 2018 Winners for 10th Annual Accelerator Pitch Event – Boston Harbor Angels." Bostonharborangels.Com. 2018.

FutureFuel announcing an $11.2 million series A round of financing on March 6, 2019[16].

THERE ARE NO BAD IDEAS

"Do you just work with anyone who signs up?" I am often asked about my startup consulting work.

"What about the people who come in with really bad ideas?"

When working with startups, it is ultimately up to the customers and the market to decide if the idea is worthwhile. My goal is to decide if the idea in its current state is investor-ready. It has to be more than just an idea. There must be a story-line and potential we can really get investors excited about. For these clients, we focus on the fundraising documents, strategy, and outreach around it.

For ideas that are not investor-ready, we figure out ways to get them there. Building out a minimal viable product or functioning prototype to test the market, gain feedback, and adapt is an excellent way to move your company forward before a capital raise.

---

16 2019. Americaninno.Com. 2019.

There are plenty of success stories that started out as what everyone considered a "bad idea." I know several investors here in Boston who were approached by Travis Kalanick of Uber in the early days with the crazy idea people would choose to share their location and jump in a car with a complete stranger—without a taxi medallion or commercial driving credentials—and pay market rates for it.

Naturally, they all said no to the investment.

SOLUTION-FIRST IDEAS

Sometimes, great discoveries that turn into successful businesses happen by accident, with solutions developed for a problem we did not know existed.

Silly Putty, the popular kids toy formed from a moldable ball of putty that can capture the form and imprints of text it touches, was invented in the 1940s by James Wright — by accident.

During World War II, the U.S. War Production Board was tasked with finding a cheaper solution to creating synthetic rubber for the government, and as one of the top scientists for General Electric, James was brought on the job. He tried various solutions of chemicals, testing hundreds of variations of key ingredients to find the perfect compound. On one of the trials, he mixed silicone oil with boric acid and found the compound acted very much like rubber. It could rebound almost 25 percent higher than a normal rubber ball, but it was soft and malleable and it could stretch to many times its original length without tearing.

It failed to meet the standards the agency had set for synthetic rubber, but James was determined to find a use for the new invention. His putty had several unique characteristics including its ability to copy the image of any printed material it was pressed upon. Through a chance encounter at a General Electric party, James Wright would find his champion in Peter Hodgson to lead the product forward to become the famous children's toy it is today. Peter's son recalls his story in an interview with the Associated Press:

"It was a thinking kid's toy," said Peter Hodgson Jr., who teaches Russian literature at UCLA. "The fact that it was a solid-liquid, and the way it behaved in your hand... Part of its weirdness is that it had no use at all. It's hard to imagine any other culture, any other country, in which this could have made sense... and nobody less eccentric than my old man could have carried it off."

Peter Hodgson, Sr. and his partner at the time, Ruth Fallgater, were attending a party hosted by a General Electric director where James Wright's putty was passed around the room. The duo ran an advertising catalog for a toy store and decided to buy some of the putty and put it in the catalog as a toy in egg-shaped cartons for $2 each, and to their pleasant surprise it sold out![17]

Peter bought the production rights to Wright's "bouncing putty" and is credited with changing the name of Nutty Putty to Silly Putty, introducing it to the public at Easter, selling it inside plastic eggs. In 1949, Silly Putty sold faster than any other toy in history at the time, with over $6 million in sales in the first year.

Peter then expanded the market and reached his adult audience almost by accident. Parents soon discovered not only could Silly Putty lift perfect images off comic pages, but it was very handy for pulling lint off of fabric as well. It was used in space with the Apollo 8 crew in 1968, where it proved effective at keeping objects in place in zero gravity. Binney & Smith, Inc., the creator of Crayola, purchased Silly Putty after Peter's death and the company estimates that more than 300 million Silly Putty eggs have sold since 1950.[18]

**

17   "Silly Putty — From Eggs to Apollo 8." 2016. ThoughtCo. 2016.
18   "Silly Putty — From Eggs to Apollo 8." 2016. ThoughtCo. 2016.

While I have yet to create a toy through random chemical reactions, I have started companies through random connections and shared interests.

On May 25, 2016, I had been operating Prepare 4 VC for about three and a half months when I received a LinkedIn request from John Lohavichan, a serial entrepreneur and former product manager in the financial sector for Thompson Reuters and CCBN.

Hi, Jason. Happy to connect. Let me know how I might help. Lately, I've been helping startups find investors and pitch early-stage customers. Best, John, read the introductory message on LinkedIn.

I quickly replied, *Hi, John, it sounds like we operate in the same arena. I help startups impress investors with professional business plans and pitch decks written from the investor's perspective. It would be good to chat and see if we have any opportunities to work together. Best, Jason.*

We connected for a call and several meetings to discuss some of the projects we had been working on. As we were discussing startup fundraising options, one particular aspect kept coming up in our conversations: the new JOBS Act regulations surrounding equity crowdfunding that would open up startup investing to the general public, not just accredited investors.

We came together along with one of John's former coworkers on a mission to build something in the equity crowdfunding space. The more we came together and researched the space, the more we saw the complexities and costs of setting up and maintaining an equity crowdfunding portal — yet there were already 25 companies registered and ready to capitalize on the new trend.

We imagined having to scroll through 25 different crowdfunding portals, using a different investor log in and password each time to sort through all of the active deals and find the best opportunities. We went through the process ourselves to test it out to find, research, and invest in the top opportunities. From this, we decided to build a platform to aggregate all of the listings, as well as provide tools to help first-time investors analyze the deals.

A startup was born.

In interviewing the users of various crowdfunding platforms, we found that a majority were focused on the impact investment philosophy: invest in only areas you believe in and support that also have the potential to make money. For some people, this meant medical devices and applications, others backed green energy and technology, while others supported small businesses and jobs in their communities like restaurants, bars, and professional services. ImpactSeeker, as the company was originally called, would help the crowd find and analyze investment opportunities across all platforms in an easily accessible format.

Ultimately, as a company, we took a scrappy, bootstrapped approach, constantly testing and iterating the idea to improve functionality. There was a growing interest in the space and crowdfunding investors were open to connecting and discussing their interests and testing out the platform, but we struggled to monetize as the team faced internal challenges that held us back (to be discussed in a later chapter). The idea itself was strong, regardless of our execution. Companies like NewChip and KingsCrowd are leading the way in aggregated crowdfunding deals. So maybe we fell into that category of having the idea for the next Uber before Uber. Only time will tell. Each problem faced in a market can create a new venture, and each challenge faced as a startup better shapes the founders into leaders for their current and future ventures.

"Passion, creativity, and resilience are the most crucial skills in business. If you've got those, you're ready to embark on the journey." — *Jo Malone, Founder of Jo Malone*

**

- Market validation is key, let the customers decide what is a good idea and what does not work.
- Startup ideas/eureka moments can come from personal challenges faced as well as business pain points. Be on the lookout for ways to tie these together in a unique solution.
- Some innovations are driven by a solution-first approach that is looking for the right target market.

GET OUT THERE AND TALK… AND LISTEN!

————

"Perfectionism is a disease. Procrastination is a disease. ACTION is the cure."

— RICHIE NORTON, AUTHOR

"The early adopters have so much information about what's working and not working with your product. In these conversations, they begin to tell you things that you have no idea were problems. Like, 'We can't use your calendar.' And I watched them try and use our interface… and it was a *train wreck*."

This train wreck was a startup, a year and a half since inception, in the middle of the famous YCombinator accelerator program. This startup had convinced YCombinator founder Paul Graham to schedule a last-minute interview for the program as the company was on its last legs.

This startup bootstrapped and survived by hand-making boxes of limited-edition cereal called Obama O's and Cap'n McCains that sold for $40 each during the 2008 Presidential Election, and this story alone of grit and perseverance got them accepted into the accelerator program[19].

The struggling startup was the Unicorn we know today as Airbnb and the quote was from co-founder Joe Gebbia at the StartupGrind Global Conference in Silicon Valley.

They had a website and a user base that was chugging along with mediocre growth and shoddy photos of property listings shot by users.

"You know, it's okay to do things early that don't scale," Paul Graham told the team in one of their advisory sessions. This short quip would ultimately change the course and projection of the company.

---

19   WIRED Staff. 2017. "Airbnb's Surprising Path to Y Combinator." WIRED. WIRED. February 21, 2017.

TEST THE WATERS

"My entrepreneurial journey to RedHead Wine started long before I was born," Marisa Sergi, the founder of the hip wine startup RedHead Wine, described her pathway to becoming a third-generation winemaker during our phone interview. We had connected through the Next Gen Summit, one of the largest networking communities for young entrepreneurs.

In 1953, Marisa's grandparents immigrated to America from Italy, bringing the tradition of making wine along with them. Marisa crushed her first grape clusters with her family as a child and fell in love with the process.

From working at the family business at L'uva Bella Winery and traveling to and working with other wineries, Marisa had developed an eye for what differentiated great wine from the rest. There was one thing missing in all the bottles she had grown to love: a true brand which appealed to mass-market Millennials. The craft beer space was rapidly growing, yet consumers still had to choose between the good stuff in fancy bottles and the cheap creatively designed boxed wine.

"My parents wanted me to spruce up the packaging, so I thought it'd be fun to have my own label on being a redhead, just kind of joking around. I decided to put a little effort into it. People buy with their eyes. So if the packaging is nice, it's definitely going to be a winner in some regard."

Marisa found through surveying, observing, and researching customers that they tend to buy labels that are simple, bold, and eye-catching. She used the redhead concept as a backbone for designing the label.

"It was just a simple project for fun while I was working at the winery," Marisa explained. "I saw my label had to be very simple and eye-catching, yet classy. So I designed the RedHead label with three simple colors: red, white, and black and established the brand. But from there, I made a wine to match my personality, sweet and spicy just like a redhead."

In 2011, Marisa attended Cornell for a Bachelor of Science in Enology and Viticulture to further her passion. This put RedHead Wine on the back burner — something for her resume rather than her career. Near the end of Marisa's college career, she was able to use her concept for RedHead in one of her classes, and the feedback was an instant success.

"I proposed that I would take the label I designed to become my capstone project, and my professors approved it. So I created a business plan for the brand and the wine-making process and ended up entering it in several business plan competitions," Marisa recalls. "And that's how I really got the ball rolling. I got a lot of feedback, especially because I was just a winemaker with an idea. I didn't take it too seriously. I did research, and it was not like I sought out to actually make it into a business. I think that light-pressured situations made it really successful."

The first competition was The Queen's Entrepreneurship Competition in Kingston, Ontario. It is a global competition that received over 200 entrants from around the globe. RedHead Wine was ranked in the top fifteen.

"So that was really exciting. Very, very exciting. So pretty much long story short, I placed at every single business plan competition I've entered in. And then I was having all that positive feedback. I realized I could have something really special, like, wow, maybe I can actually do this as my full-time job and really try to make this work."

The $5,000 from the business plan competitions certainly helped kick things off, but Marisa claims the biggest thing she won from these competitions was the free knowledge and advice from mentors, judges, and audience members who helped point her in the right direction.

After graduating in 2015, Marisa took a job at E&J Gallo Wine Gallery, the largest privately-owned winery in the world. RedHead Wine was not forgotten; Marisa wanted some stability before launching into full start-up mode.

As Marisa's idea came to life with the new designs and recipe, her family agreed to launch one of the RedHead Wine designs and products under their business to test out the market and avoid the conflicts with her job she would face launching the brand herself. It was an instant success, gaining immediate traction and in August 2016, Marisa decided to quit her job to pursue RedHead Wines under her own company full-time.

"I had been approached by an investor. He was willing to put a decent amount of money into the business, but I turned it down because I wasn't ready. I was just out of college and was working for E&J Gallo. So, it was definitely an issue. I couldn't take the money or else I would be breaking contracts with my employer. Since going full-time with RedHead Wine, I've raised some money through friends and family as well as winning a $5,000 grant from a woman in entrepreneurship group. I'm thinking about going to the next step at this point. I might be starting a second company, with a person I met through Cornell University who is in the beverage space. We're potentially going to raise money through that. I'll be kind of piggybacking off that experience to really make a solid case for RedHead Wine to get funding."

After the launch and raising some friends and family investments as well as grants, the startup hustle was in full force.

She had to do one of the hardest things in fundraising: turn down several offers from equity investors with too low of a valuation. Marisa split time between the office managing the business side, her facilities managing the product development, and launching two new product lines. The biggest moment of validation came for her when a distributor agreed to come on board, accelerating the sales cycle and scale.

"When I pitched a distributor to carry RedHead, what I didn't know at the time was that obtaining a distributor is very, very challenging because they have so many products, they want value from working with you. They want to know that if they take you on, they're going to make money. So, with that being said, I picked a distributor and got them to accept the deal by representing RedHead in the market alongside their efforts, and I'm in nearly every chain in the region now. Every time I get an appointment, they accept my product, which is very hard to do. I pitched Walmart. I'm in Walmart now and most of the big stores in my territory. We are also in three states now. I'm not only selling in Ohio, but I'm also selling in Pennsylvania and West Virginia, and I have not been discontinued at any stores yet!

"This industry is built on relationships, so it's all about the sit-down conversation, the vibe, the chemistry. The two distributors I have were really casual, but depending on who you're dealing with, it could be very formal. My other distributor in

West Virginia actually sought us out. They heard our products were excellent and they drove to the winery for a tour and they sampled the products and they signed us on the spot right there."

Pitching her distributor came with the same anxiety and weight as pitching an investor, knowing this one relationship could take her business to the next level. The main difference, as Marisa noted in our interview, was the style of conversations. Investor meetings were more formal, with some small talk then straight down to business while the distributor built a causal relationship discussing wines and travel with her as they got into the sales and distribution plans.

Marisa's story continues as she expands her outreach and connections, establishing the RedHead Wine brand with even more major players in the space.

**

You've taken the first step, had your eureka moment, and thought of the idea that is going to revolutionize how we eat, sleep, shop, date, or do business. You have a vision that, with the right time, capital, and execution behind it will become the next big thing.

Where do you start?

Some startups, like Marisa Sergi's RedHead Wine, are born out of business plan competitions and a soft launch under their family business that proves wildly successful. Before investing all of your resources into your newfound passion and asking others to do the same, it is important to run smaller tests to validate your idea.

The minimal viable product (MVP) is any early-stage version of what your company will offer that has the bare minimum of functionality to get feedback and validation from future customers. These can come in all shapes and sizes from mockups, to Kickstarter campaigns and business plan competitions, to manual validation of automated services and licensing deals. The key here is to scale down the startup costs to delay quitting your job and fundraising until you have your proof of concept from customers.

The most important part? Just getting out there and getting feedback to learn from as you venture forward.

DO THINGS EARLY THAT DON'T SCALE

It is easy to get lost in the hype of what seems like overnight successes in high profile startups, but these companies also started as scrappy founders hustling to test their ideas and build a business. Just like Marisa building up her business from a design and an idea to where it is today, even billion-dollar businesses like Airbnb start from scrappy founders with a vision.

"It was the summer of 2006, I have my life spread out on the sidewalk in Providence, Rhode Island, and I'm selling all my things at a yard sale in front of my house before I move out to the West Coast, to San Francisco," Joe Gebbia, Co-Founder of Airbnb recounts the pre-founding story leading up to the company at the 2019 StartupGrind Global Conference. "It's toward the end of the day, I'm getting kind of tired and this guy pulls up in a red Miata. He looks at my stuff, a T-shirt over here, piece of art over there, and we get to talking. It turns out he drove cross-country to join the peace corps, stopping in Providence, and didn't know a soul in the area. And it just kind of came out of my mouth, 'You want to grab a drink tonight?'"

Joe went out for a drink with this stranger he had just met, and they had a great conversation lasting all night. It was getting late, and Joe asked the waiter for the check and followed up by asking the other guy where he was staying that night, when Joe found out he had nowhere to go.

"Do I offer to host this guy? I mean, I just met him. He doesn't seem that crazy, he's going into the peace corps, but who knows..." Joe recalls the thoughts racing through his head that night, "And before I know it, I said, 'How about I let you stay on an air mattress in my living room.' And so 15 minutes later, I had set him up and I go back to my bedroom to fall asleep or try to fall asleep… I'm lying in my bed, my eyes are wide open and looking at the ceiling going, 'Oh, my God!, What have I done? There's a stranger in my living room.' I get up and tiptoe over to the door, lock the bedroom door. Turns out he was totally fine, we got breakfast the next morning, he went off to the peace corps, sent me postcards, and we are still friends to this day."

Not knowing it at the time, Joe's experience of sharing his air mattress with a complete stranger he had just met and became friends with ultimately shaped the vision for Airbnb. It seemed unnatural to him at first, coming from a world where we are taught as small children not to talk to strangers and our media is filled with violence, but once he had the experience, he got great joy out of helping others and making a new friend in the process. The story and his air mattress came along with him as Joe packed his belongings and drove out to San Francisco to start a new company with his friend and roommate Brian Chesky, the future co-founder and CEO of Airbnb.

"A year had gone by, Brian and I were roommates in San Francisco and the rent went up beyond our means. We had a math problem—we quit our jobs to be entrepreneurs and here was a rent check we can't pay, we are on the verge of getting evicted, what do we do?"

Joe and Brian's saving grace was a design conference coming to the city of San Francisco. It wiped out all available hotels that weekend and they saw every hotel website had sold out rooms. They looked over their apartment and saw an opportunity. They bought two more air mattresses, setting up all three in the living room and made a posting online to sell the spots to incoming travelers, complete with a homemade breakfast.

It was a success, bringing in $1,000 for the weekend and making three new friends in the process. And with that, Airbnb was born.

Joe and Brian did not immediately jump on the vision and start the company after their experience. They had been working through several venture ideas those first few years and kept searching for their big idea. It wasn't until both of them were traveling home for the holidays and the most exciting story they kept telling their friends and family was of the weekend that they rented out the apartment to strangers for $1,000 and made new friends that they realized the power of what they could build.

People either loved or hated the idea but all provided valuable feedback which would shape the vision of what would become Airbnb. Joe and Brian came back together, shared their experience and decided this was it— their mission and vision would be to create a community of bed and breakfasts from everyday people's homes: Air Bed and Breakfast or Airbnb.

They launched a website, continuously coding and updating it and were growing in several regions around the US, but like most startups, they went through growing pains. Their key moment of advice came from Paul Graham of YCombinator, who said, "It's okay to do things that don't scale," and solve issues outside of programming.

They took the lesson to heart.

New York was their biggest market at the time with thirty listings, and they looked at the photos in the city and saw the quality of the photos were terrible: blurry images in unclean apartments. Joe had a background in photography, so he bought a quality camera and headed to New York with Brian to meet the Airbnb homeowners there and offer to take free photos of their apartments. During these sessions, they would chat with the owners, who would share depths of information and insight on their experiences and insights.

"The early adopters have so much information about what's working and not working with your product… In these conversations, they begin to tell you things that you have no idea were problems. Like, 'We can't use your calendar.' And I watched them try and use our interface, and it was a train wreck."

Joe continued the interview process with strong insights from a variety of customers. One member even kept a notebook of ideas he had for the Airbnb experience that he shared with the team to take back with them and use.

Upon flying back to San Francisco, they quickly updated the features based on the user insights and followed up with each one to show their ideas had been taken into account, building upon the website and scaling it for success. Throughout the process, the founders and the team continue to make it a key part of their mission to listen to customer feedback in scaling for success.

SCALING THE IDEA WITH THE BUSINESS

One of my early clients with Prepare 4 VC in the real estate technology industry shares a similar story of shaping the company and vision around customer feedback. I connected with entrepreneur Jarred Kessler as he was looking for help with a pitch deck around his idea at the time for a site that connected property buyers and sellers, leveraging a premium domain they had under agreement for Property.com.

Jarred was an experienced executive in the real estate industry and knew the business aspects in out and out, but the product was still just in the idea phase. As I worked on the deck, we brainstormed ways to receive a higher perceived level of traction and validation for the investor pitch and showcase the market need. We developed an in-depth survey of homeowners' needs, seeking outside opinions to ensure our questions were unbiased, and then we launched a blind survey to collect data from hundreds of homeowners.

The response was powerful in that it validated some level of interest in the platform, with a high level of interest in a few features that were mentioned throughout the survey. The overall idea of another marketplace application under a powerful domain was underwhelming to most users with Zillow and RedFin already in the market, but people loved two of the key features including being able to take offers on their home without officially listing it for sale and the proposed sell & stay model to access the equity in your home and stay as a permanent tenant.

We took the data and transformed the focus of the brand around these two key features, with Jarred's new brand Easy-Knock. The innovative approach driven by consumer desire led to a strong seed round of financing and the company quickly launched the platform the beginning of 2017.

As the company proceeded, listening to customer feedback remained a cornerstone of Jarred's management. The Easy-Knock Sell & Stay model of tapping into the homeowner's equity and allowing them to stay as a tenant was gaining significant traction and became the focus of the platform. The company redesigned the technology and marketing around this approach and has raised an additional several million dollars in follow on equity financing as well as a $100 million credit line for transactions.

"EasyKnock's vision is to reimagine and recreate homeownership," Jarred stated in a 2019 Forbes interview. "We can save homeowners from having to leave their home in a time where they simply don't want to[20]."

"If you are working on a product that's going to be consumer-facing, then feedback is invaluable. You should be out there being brave and talking to people and asking for feedback as much as possible."

—EMILY BROOKE, CO-FOUNDER OF BLAZE

**

---

20 Rogers, Bruce. 2019a. "EasyKnock Aims to Simplify Home Equity Finance." *Forbes*, January 8, 2019.

VENTURING FORWARD TAKEAWAYS:

- Feedback is king in shaping your startup.
- It's okay to do things early that do not scale.
- There are ways to test the waters and validate a concept before jumping all in with both feet and scaling for mass-market adoption.

FINDING YOUR
CHAMPION

"My advice is to focus on the importance of forging a long-term relationship, whether with colleagues, partners, or customers. It is often easy to get caught up in short-term decisions."

—SHEILA LIRIO MARCELO, FOUNDER OF CARE.COM

You hear a radio advertisement for a new restaurant downtown, but when you go online to check it out there are no reviews yet. Do you take the plunge?

You click the Facebook advertisement on a really cool gadget that you get excited about, but you click on their Facebook page and the company only has seven likes. Do you still trust them and buy their product?

Some readers here are ready to jump right in; entrepreneurs as a breed are curious at heart and tend to be early adopters. However, 91 percent of consumers regularly or occasionally read online reviews, with 84 percent trusting reviews as much as a personal recommendation[21].

In the digital age, it is becoming increasingly powerful to find early adopters and advocates to jump on board and test out your business who can spread the message through word of mouth—champions of the product who tell their friends, write reviews and recommendations, or rally investors around your cause. Every day, the number of companies that "have investors lined up" and are waiting for a lead investor seems to grow as startups look to find their champion.

Samantha Zirkin, the founder of retail technology company Point93, has a simple solution to finding the right advisors, customers, and partners to champion her project: *Do your homework.*

21 Bloem, Craig. 2017. "84 Percent of People Trust Online Reviews As Much As Friends. Here's How to Manage What They See." Inc.Com. Inc. July 31, 2017.

"I wasn't technical and went to a bunch of technology meetups in hopes of finding a Chief Technology Officer (CTO) and I learned that this guy Brian Behlendorf runs a company called Hyperledger. He is a legend; he invented Apache and he was the CTO for the World Economic Forum. He did a whole lot of other amazing things and everybody said such wonderful things about this guy. So I went on his blog and I saw where he was speaking and then I read and read through his background so that I was very familiar with it by the time I met up with him. I went to this conference he was speaking at in Vegas, and I *accidentally* bumped into him and talked all about his work. We became friends, and now he's my advisor."

Samantha did not wait for her champion to appear; she created her opportunities. She took the lead and showed she was ready to do whatever it takes to venture forward.

SALES FIRST INNOVATION

"We never really set out to start a company. I was just a driven intern looking to stand out on the day-to-day work and make a difference." Deepak Atyam is the founder and CEO of Tri-D Dynamics, a startup that creates Cold Metal Fusion printers for ultra-fast manufacturing.

Deepak attended the University of California, San Diego for a Bachelor's in Aerospace, Aeronautical, and Astronautical

Engineering and started his first internship at NASA in 2010, interning at NASA every summer throughout college. NASA spent millions of dollars in capital each year on maintenance and manufacturing for its space program and was looking for ways to reduce costs without compromising safety and quality.

"3D printing was starting to get big at the time in the plastics space, but no one had really cracked the code of how to 3D print usable metal objects. Thinking this would be the future and the answer to NASA's problems, we set out to find 3D printed solutions," said Deepak.

Each summer and throughout the school year, Deepak worked diligently on designing and printing rocket engines using advanced metal 3D printing equipment. He joined the University's Moxie Center for Entrepreneurship to take advantage of additional resources as a startup. As they progressed, the team Deepak worked with at NASA began funding the project as a revenue stream into what was becoming Tri-D Dynamics, a startup that was forming with an engaged customer even before it was a company.

"We used our traction to enter several business plan competitions throughout our time at UC San Diego. Honestly, we were just joining to get free space at the school to continue our work, but we ended up winning over $100K in prizes from the competitions we entered. That was a tremendous boost to launch our startup story," Deepak recalls.

As Tri-D Dynamics continued to gain traction, the team realized they would need to transition their application to a broader market, as there were just several main customers in the space market they could target. They decided to raise a round of capital to expand their efforts.

"I had no idea how to raise capital, so I researched everything I could find and read reports on the best investors to target for our type of company. I cold emailed every investor I could, with brief targeted messages on why we stood out from the crowd and it was really successful. Soon I was on the phone with Adam Draper and his fund who ended up investing $500K into our business after several meetings and this really accelerated our growth."

Adam Draper is the son of famous billionaire venture capitalist Tim Draper, and the founder of his own venture fund Boost VC. He is a fourth-generation venture capitalist, a two-time successful entrepreneur, and his deal flow is tremendous. But in a venture capital world where introductions are king, Deepak was able to crack into a leading investor through cold emails. Simple, concise emails that presented the value of the opportunity, why the team was in the optimal position to venture forward, and how Adam Draper's investment would create a return on investment for the growth of the company and Adam's team of investors.

Deepak also raised additional funds through National Science Foundation grants and several individual Angel investors as Tri-D Dynamics began to expand. The team stretched out the budget as far as they could, even living in Deepak's co-founders' parents' house and spreading out a ten thousand annual salary to kick things off until the profits grew.

"We knew we were onto something big and having the support of our customers from the start led us to where we are today, investing in growth and scaling for mass-market adoption."

**

Another founder I connected with through the NextGen Summit network, Atisha Patel, echoes the importance of finding a core user to champion and test the product. She is a biomedical engineer by trade with background work at renowned institutions like Novartis Pharmaceuticals and the University of Pennsylvania.

"I have always been a problem solver at heart," said Atisha. "I have kept a word document since high school with ideas of what I wanted to change in the world and took an engineering approach to it with notes and diagram doodles.

At Drexel University, we had the opportunity to do a rotation in surgery and emergency medicine, which was the catalyst for my interest in health tech, a field that did not exist back then. Our job as biomedical engineers was to work with the doctors and staff to bridge a vital gap between healthcare and technology—hence the recent boom in the health tech industry, which is predicted to hit $504 billion by 2025. I dabbled in several different spaces including one, which was in blockchain, Atom Mine, that grew out of a need my co-founders and I discovered at a networking event, which would reward users for completing task-based challenges allowing users to sell their own data. I learned quickly that I am not merely math and science-oriented, but strategic and operations were innate skills. Without a true business background and to hone into those skills, I worked with a couple other startups in hydroponics and startup consulting before founding my current startups Noticare and Teenpreneur."

Atom Mine dissolved after 10 months of her joining because of conflicts between the co-founders and served as a learning experience for her next ventures. Atisha continued to capture new ideas in her startup journal and used her experiences to weed out and fine-tune the next steps. Less than a year later, in March of 2017, she was struck by the big idea for NotiCare.

"The idea of NotiCare stemmed from an experience my best friend and now co-founder had volunteering as a NICU baby cuddler. She called me asking if we could get drinks to hear my perspective on a situation she had observed earlier that day. She made several observations but what stood out most was how many times throughout the day nurses would receive calls from concerned parents to check in on their newborn." All of the phones were constantly on hold as the nurses shifted between their routines and tasks managing the babies in the NICU and fielding phone calls.

There had to be a better way.

Atisha and her co-founder, Christina Flory, dug in deeper on the issue and found a widespread problem among hospitals around the country: 84 minutes of the average 12-hour shift was spent talking with family members by phone instead of caring for patients. Several members of the same family would separately call to request the same information. Nurses would have to take a message for the doctor on the case but when the doctor called back, they may get a full voicemail box. "The whole process was quite antiquated."

NotiCare was born as an application for real-time patient updates to quickly keep all primary contacts informed throughout the day.

"Being involved in the hospital already gave us a leg up in testing and launching NotiCare. My co-founder and I retained our full-time jobs as well, which allowed us the flexibility to scale, test, and iterate on the concept without rushing into funding or revenue too early."

She stressed the importance of stability and bootstrapping first as you grow and scale your business. Her goal is to raise capital and scale the platform when the traction is right, but her focus, for now, is on growing the platform and interest as much as possible prior to a fundraise. Even the development work on the application itself was accelerated by bootstrapped development. Atisha and Christina, both alumni of Drexel University, sponsored a technology development project for the school in which a group of students in the computer science program was tasked with creating and upgrading early versions of the communication system.

Each step of the way, the NotiCare team has found lean startup ways to test and innovate on efficiently while they establish their presence and meet customer needs. The company is two years in and continues to gain traction.

"The Philadelphia entrepreneurial community has given me a lot and shortly after launching NotiCare, we decided we wanted to find a way to give back. For the last two summers, we have run a one-week accelerator program to teach teenage students interested in entrepreneurship how to leverage their creative ideas and start companies. Teenpreneur is our startup program we created to help the community, and to be honest, I learn as much from the students as they do from us. It's been a great experience."

FEEDBACK THROUGH EVENTS

Just like many of our founders so far were able to focus on market tests and validation to prove out their business before funding, a process known as bootstrapping, our story of ImpactSeeker continues with quick tests and iterations. John, the co-founder I had met through LinkedIn, along with his old colleague who had become our third co-founder, and I continued as we focused on quick market tests and iterating our path forward.

All three co-founders were non-technical but each had a basic understanding of how software was built. We found our perfect toolset in Bubble, a code-free solution to build database platforms for a low monthly fee. We needed to connect the workflow of the site together and learn to build the system, but using code-free technology enabled us to avoid high development costs and leverage APIs and plug-ins, which were included in the subscription.

John initially took the lead on development while we focused on the data, compiling all of the crowdfunding campaigns to date and lists of those who had established themselves as crowdfunding investors. We would divide up tasks and research, using productivity tools like Trello and Google Docs to organize categories of crowdfunding sites, startups, and investors as we gained insight into the new marketplace. We were constantly chatting with other crowdfunding investors from the sites through LinkedIn and by phone or in person, trying to capture their biggest needs into our product, and the ImpactSeeker team would meet in person once per week to go over results and discuss the next phase of work.

As we began to see this project coming to life from an idea to a business, I brought up the hard topic of equity allocation early on. I had offered to take less equity as I continued to work on Prepare 4 VC projects to provide income as we proceeded, but they agreed that my venture connections and startup network would be a worthy resource and we could all proceed as equal partners in the firm. After several months, we launched our version 1 alpha site to the public with the goal of sprint iterations based on feedback. We first promoted to small forums on and to our networks, making initial contacts on the B2B side, as well as with crowdfunding sites and events groups.

One day, at our weekly meeting at our third co-founder's house, he gave us the news that would shift our startup trajectory.

"I was just offered a full-time position in a senior vice president role in a product development group. The job is in Dallas, but it's a normal nine-to-five so I will work nights and weekends on ImpactSeeker."

While the move took us by surprise—neither of us knew he was looking for a new role—we were optimistic about the future and had known plenty of entrepreneurs who juggled their nine-to-five (work), with their five-to-nine (their startup or passion project). Over the next two months, we continued pushing forward, but John and I were able to really drive the company forward while most of our weekly meetings were now spent catching up our other founder and asking for input. The role he was playing was an important position in any startup, but it was becoming the responsibilities of an advisor with the equity of a founder.

As we struggled to find product market fit and grow from our core test users, we faced several differences of opinions on how to proceed in our next iterations and tests, complicated further by the fact we had vastly different contributions occurring for the same 33 percent equity. In the end, our nimble structure proved even the team itself had to be tested quickly and efficiently, and we shut down ImpactSeeker. John and I left to find a new niche in the space to launch our next idea, developing what would become Mattervest as new partners. We found a market that was extremely open to exploring the new space and engaging with our concept, pivoting to the cryptocurrency and token marketplace.

Our timing was perfect to start.

We hit the boom of excitement into the cryptocurrency space. We set up a meetup group for crypto events and filled the room within two weeks of promotion: Complete strangers were interested in what we were doing and how they could learn about the cryptocurrency offers out there in this new financial frontier.

I began developing the site with John as we both wore every startup hat. We moved into a coworking space, Coalition, in the heart of downtown Boston, and we kicked into full gear. Our engagement was rising, we were tracking how people were using the site and seeing what buttons and topics users interacted with, what empty spaces they tried to click that we needed to fix and we were quickly iterating and optimizing.

The event group became our platform for finding our market and testing with users: a group of Mattervest Champions we created as we worked to find larger partnerships for integrations and develop a monetization strategy.

Unfortunately, the timing was not *entirely* perfect. We were in the swing of the craze of the ICO market, which was booming in the US, based on the thesis that cryptocurrencies were commodities that could be bought and sold and redeemable with a utility value for goods or services. The SEC and Massachusetts regulators, in particular, did not agree with that sentiment and started cracking down and shutting down many of the cryptocurrency companies that were being publicized. Our model for the website to show all the cryptocurrency deals available no longer worked and after several quick pivots, we ultimately shut the company down as well.

"In a way, failure saved us both times. In one instance, the failure of ImpactSeeker saved us from regret of each doing 50 percent of the work and giving away 33 percent of the equity on a successful venture, while if Mattervest had become a huge success, we would have been the spotlight example with hefty fines that our peers in the cryptocurrency market were receiving to shift founders away from this model of fundraising," John said. "I wouldn't have traded in either venture. We learned so much that we both use in current ventures."

John recently launched a platform TrustFuss.com that provides warranty information and reviews on its first target market, camping gear. He is an avid hiker, has found a community of people with similar frustrations and needs in the hiking community, and is taking our lessons from the financial space to bring TrustFuss to the market.

There are many ways to test and grow along your entrepreneurial journey. The phrase "fail early and often" is key to startup success. If you can take feedback, mistakes, and successes to build your companies on top of, every iteration will help gain more traction. In the digital age, we are able to develop ideas into reality faster than ever before and must make sure to use that to our advantage as we move our companies forward.

**

Over the last several years, I have found many great networking events around the Boston Startup and event scene to leverage. As we relaunched Mattervest to focus on a space that was gaining even more traction quicker than crowdfunding, crypto and ICO investments, we took as many presentation opportunities as we could for quick access to rooms filled with potential users.

We presented at Boston New Technology to over 100 attendees at a monthly event that showcases new trending startups to the Boston Tech community, receiving great feedback from the audience, signups on our platforms, and connections with investors from 1000 Angels and other investment groups we could establish a relationship with early on.

Additionally, I leveraged my Babson College Graduate school connection to participate in the annual Rocket Pitch event, where every presenter is given three minutes to pitch to an audience who all have feedback cards to submit their ideas to the founders on how to move their companies forward. The feedback was phenomenal, and we met some other great entrepreneurs I have worked with on their fundraising efforts since as well.

In my current roles at Prepare 4 VC and investment groups EQx Fund, Equity Venture Partners, and Boston Harbor Angels, I regularly attend networking and pitch events, as well as direct other startups to organizers I have connected with at these groups.

I have been involved with the Hackers and Hustlers meetup group, established to host an entrepreneur's pitch for feedback and to make connections with the Hackers on the tech side and the Hustlers on the business side. I have judged the Hult International Business School Business plan competition, reviewing a variety of startups built throughout a yearlong grad program, and have seen similar great programs and competitions around the city.

There are startup events almost every night of the week here, and there are many great speakers presenting at fireside chat and panel events to share their story with the startup community. One of my favorite fireside chat events was StartupGrind, a local chapter of the Global Startup networking community with 650 chapters worldwide reaching two million entrepreneurs. After attending several events with the previous director, the chapter leader moved away from the city and I applied to take over the chapter, being accepted by the corporate StartupGrind team to lead events in May of 2018. Each month, we host a fireside chat with leaders in the local startup scene, and all of the chapters from around the world come together each February in Silicon Valley for the StartupGrind Global conference with 8000 attendees in the startup ecosystem.

Whether you are looking to pitch your company for feedback, gain users, learn from experienced entrepreneurs and investors, or network for your next co-founder, there is an event for you in your local startup ecosystem. If one doesn't exist, there are resources like global networking communities and Meetup.com that let you create and launch an organization of your own.

SEEKING OUT YOUR CHAMPION

"The goal is to drive profit and optimize operations for retailers. It's also good for us as shoppers. It's going to save us all lots of money and here's how it's going to work," Samantha Zirkin explained during one of our Startup Grind fireside chats. She is the founder and CEO of Point 93, a blockchain-powered shopping application that stores and matches consumers' willingness to pay for particular items with store sales for automatic purchase.

"We have all seen those popup ads that say *Save 20 percent if you add your email* and so the retailers have thought about the value of each email they add to their system. I talked with retailers and asked them what else they need to know and found out that size data is super important. They all said they would pay a ton to know how many of each size they need in the store, so they won't run out of smalls or have too many X-larges left over, etc. Inventory and lost sales cost them a lot of money."

Samantha did her homework, interviewing as many retailers and customers as possible, as well as completing industry research that found 50 percent of dresses bought online were returned. She collected all of this data as she worked on her solution for Point 93: Retailers want data and are willing to pay for it, consumers care about privacy and do not want their information shared without permission, inventory and returns are a huge problem, and incentives seem to work.

"As these ideas morphed together, I imagined a service where the store would offer discounts for promising not to return the item, for providing data, and for any other information the store has a clear value for. We serve as the intermediary, keeping the data in the hands of the consumer to decide who they want to share their information with or revoke access to."

Initial feedback was strong, and Samantha began to assemble a team to help build Point 93. She taught herself to code an initial version from programs like code.org, but she soon realized that this should not be her focus if she was also running the business and started to search for developers and CTO to come on board. So, Samantha ventured to all of the technology meetups she could find in hopes of finding a Chief Technology Officer (CTO). While networking at these events, she had heard several people reference Brian Behlendorf, the former founder or Apache and the CTO of the World Economic Forum. His current company, Hyperledger, was becoming a leader in the blockchain space and Samantha vowed to herself that she would meet him and learn from him.

"So I went on his blog and I saw he was speaking and then I read and read through his background so that I was very familiar with the time I met up with him. I went to this conference he was speaking at in Vegas and I *accidentally* bumped into him and talk all about his work. We became friends and now he's my advisor."

Samantha was determined to learn from the best and made it a point to reach out and interact with the advisors she wanted.

"And similarly, Jimmy Wales who runs Wikipedia, I think to myself that's the guy I want to meet. I had some questions on his work and we connected from there. These people are accessible. I also was on the phone with a Nobel Prize winner, a guy named Daniel Kahneman—you should all read his book *Thinking Fast and Slow,* amazing! The guy won the Nobel Prize and it took one cold email of, 'Hey, I really admire your work,' and a deep discussion I engaged him on to become close connections."

Samantha makes knowledge, learning, and networking an integral part of her routine as she builds the company. Her application has been tested in private betas in several major retail brands and is getting ready for the public launch. She makes sure to take active observations on consumer behaviors and adjust the technology accordingly.

"You guys may have suspected that men are different than women, totally different, but men really reacted to shopping in a whole different way and like reactive bargaining in a different way. For example, men see things more as commodities, like, 'I want to buy a white shirt,' whereas most women think by brands; 'I have to have this Vitas cotton shirt,' and it's not interchangeable. We found that people abandoned the app at different times. Some would find it a cognitive burden to have pricing options back and forth too many times, so we adjusted our algorithms for smoother transactions with fewer touchpoints." The company is continually adapting to feedback and advice as the brand and application takes on the future of retail.

∗∗

On a personal level, I can definitely relate the power of leveraging connections with authors and experts in fields you are passionate about. It always helps when you have read someone's work and can have a deep discussion and ask them for further insights.

About a year ago, during the Angel Capital Association conference in Boston, I hopped into an Uber Pool for my ride home. Just as I got in, we were connected with a second rider and pulled around the corner to pick him up. I recognized him instantly from both the conference and from the cover of his book I had read.

David S. Rose is the founder and CEO of Gust, one of the main platforms Angel Groups and accelerators around the United States use for managing deal flow and startup applications. He is an investor himself, organizing the New York Angels group and has written one of the most famous books in the field entitled *Angel Investing*.

I knew two things as soon as he stepped in:

1) He did not need to be taking a shared Uber back to the hotel to save a few dollars and must be down to earth.

2) I definitely wanted to speak to him and learn from him.

We had a conversation about the book and his thoughts on angel investing and what separates the great startup deals from the rest. I gained a wealth of knowledge from a simple car ride, and it only happened because I had read his book, recognized him, and knew enough to talk and ask questions.

**

"Wonder what your customer really wants? Ask. Don't tell."
–Lisa Stone, BlogHer Co-Founder and CEO

VENTURING FORWARD TAKEAWAYS:

- Find an eager customer early and work to solve their needs.
- Make yourself known to the people you want to connect with, read their books, attend their events, or host events of your own.
- Timing can be a blessing and a curse. Be nimble and adaptability while protecting your startup from risk where you can.

THE CIRCLE OF STARTUP LIFE

———

"Don't worry about failure; you only have to be right once."

—DREW HOUSTON, DROPBOX CO-FOUNDER AND CEO

"Obviously running a business is hard. But for me, I looked at that as a problem that was worth trying to solve. And as I dug deeper, I realized that 90 percent of startups were failing, and I wanted to figure out why," Kyle Heron, founder of Sieo explained in our interview.

A 90 percent failure rate!

Imagine that in any other position. You are a teacher and 90 percent of your students failed the state test. *Looks like you'd be out of a job.*

Imagine shooting 10 percent of your shots in basketball or dropping 9 out of 10 passes in football. *You are certainly riding the bench the rest of the game if not off the team.*

Yet in the startup world, we accept that 9 out of 10 companies fail, and yet the vision, passion, and belief we have that we can be in that select group of successful entrepreneurs drives us forward.

Failures and successes should be embraced to take the key lessons into your next venture or job. There has been a recent push to embrace the act of failure as a learning experience with events like the global meetup group "F*ck Up Nights" where entrepreneurs share their mistakes in hopes of helping the audience avoid the same traps in the future, and a Boston-based Podcast *Failure: The Podcast* that interviews employees and founders to share failure stories every entrepreneur can learn from.

Experienced founders have made mistakes and learned the ropes for their second venture and seeking out advice and stories from seasoned entrepreneurs can get you an even higher leg up on the competition.

GROWING PAINS

"We were a team built on hustling and grinding every day with every sale. We had no guidelines or goals on how things should be done, we just learned what worked for us," Trey Bowles recalled. Trey, now a renowned entrepreneur and Chairman of the Dallas Entrepreneurship Center, entered the world of entrepreneurship in 2001 at age 24 as the first hire at peer-to-peer file-sharing giant Morpheus. As the first hire, within the first six months, Trey was asked to take on a slew of roles, which led to him launching a new sales force as the company began to gain traction.

"One day in a meeting with the founders, I presented the sales numbers and conversion rates, which I now know were about three times higher than all of our competitors in the industry. I asked if they were okay figures, not knowing where we should be in our sales efforts. We were just out there each day giving it our all," said Trey.

On a limited startup budget, Trey put together a team of interns from a local university, taking them through the ropes of the software and the features that sell, calling potential customers and converting sales. Over a few months, the salesforce of interns turned into an all-star team under Trey's leadership. They had very high conversion rates, and customers were signing up left and right. Everything was going great and the team had a strong routine until one day Trey came in and found that no one was in the office, all of the desks were empty, and no one was attending to the phones. He looked at his calendar. It was August 27th, and all of his summer interns had gone back to school.

"It was one of those moments that just hits you in the fast-paced startup environment," Trey recalled. "I was riding high on our traction and recent success, and suddenly snapped down to earth that we were still a startup relying on an intern salesforce to scale, and we could lose our traction at any time."

Morpheus faced ups and downs along the road to establishing itself as one of the leading peer-to-peer file-sharing services in the world. As it grew to its peak in 2002, over one million people per day were sharing files, trading movies, songs, and software on the platform. As the company worked to support increased demand, Morpheus extended the accounts payable further for its licensing partners and delayed payments. One particular vendor, Kaza BV, was particularly unhappy with the late payments and threatened to discontinue the service.

"We didn't think anything of it and felt like we were on top of the world, with the cards in our hand. We were integrated into their software already and customers loved us," Trey explained in our interview. "It took the team by shock when we checked the usage statistics the next day and found we had lost every single user overnight."

Kaza had issued a mandatory software upgrade to all users on their platform, which included a new software package without Morpheus and wiped out the connections to the user base. The company never recovered from the incident and entered long stages of legal disputes with several of its clients, which eventually would force the company into bankruptcy.

"I have been an entrepreneur ever since this experience and the biggest aspect for me is that every failure or success can help not only my own ventures but also help the startups around me. Why should we all have to make the same pitfalls when we can learn from each other to get ahead?"

Trey has taken the idea of learning from past experiences even further by dedicating himself to several mission-driven organizations that mentor and mold young entrepreneurs. He ran the Texas Chapter of Startup America from 2012 to 2014, launching in seven locations with varied demographic settings to target the needs to each local startup community. The goal was simple, yet powerful: let entrepreneurs learn from the mistakes their mentors made in the past.

Currently, Trey runs the Dallas Entrepreneurship Center, which he co-founded in 2013 with a similar mission of mentoring entrepreneurs into investment-ready companies. Since the launch of the organization, the impact on the community has been tremendous, amounting to a $130 million + economic impact on the Greater Dallas Community.

ENTREPRENEUR-AS-A-SERVICE

"I realized that 90 percent of startups were failing, and I wanted to figure out why," Kyle Heron, founder of Sieo explained in our interview. "And so I spent the summer after my junior year in college, just really digging into this startup failure rate and why the entrepreneurial framework that existed was not supporting startups appropriately. And ultimately what that led me to do was come together with a couple other guys who I had previously partnered with, and we collectively started a company called Sieo (the phonetic spelling of CEO). The goal was its tagline: To help startups start up. Our real mission was to redefine the way that you started a business and to systematize the process of taking an idea and turning it into something that's actually revenue-generating." Kyle Heron, another entrepreneur who decided to take his learnings in the daily startup grind and share it with others. The former founder and CEO of Sieo was on a mission.

How did his entrepreneurial journey begin? Kyle always gives credit to his parents for giving him two different sides of the entrepreneurial formula. His mother was what Kyle described as a hustler with a hard work ethic, waking up at

5:00 AM every day, raising three kids while running a full-time corporate job. His father had always worked in non-profits and philanthropy and really encouraged Kyle to chase his passion and do what he loved doing. Kyle first dove into entrepreneurship when he was 12 years old and realized he knew how computers worked much better than some of the elderly women in the neighborhood.

"I was literally shipping computer hardware and software to the grandmas in my neighborhood. I know there was a woman down the street and an older lady who wanted to order a printer online, so I would order it for her. I charged her a little extra for the process and before I knew it, I figured out what a margin looked like. With projects like that, I really chased that entrepreneurial path in informal ways up until I was about 18, when I started what I consider to be my first real company."

Kyle's first real company was called Beats for Better, a concert production company that started because he simply wanted to follow his passion for music.

"I wanted to do something I love, and I knew that I loved music. I was the type of kid who had headphones in every day. I just have always found music to be a really incredible way to escape reality and remove yourself from your day to day of idiosyncrasies. And so I created Beats for Better with the intention of giving independent artists an opportunity to perform and have their voices heard. I'm based out of LA, so it was a perfect scene to start that company, and I ran that company for about two years, facing some challenges near the end."

Kyle explains that as the business struggled and his passion faltered, he was so hungry to learn how to build a business he kept it going as a learning experience. "I never really knew where to start to be honest. This was before I knew what accelerators were. This is before I knew how to approach an angel. This is before I even knew about what it means to become incorporated. I didn't only bootstrap it in terms of funding, but I bootstrapped it certainly in knowledge, and when all was said and done, it ended up being a big learning experience for me more than anything else."

In Kyle's next venture, he joined forces with a few friends from school at Chapman University and they started a company called Filter Shit Out. The premise was similar to Yelp with localized attractions and destinations while including a unique machine-learning algorithm behind it. The platform would curate suggestions of things to do based on a variety of data points, social media interaction with the app and beyond.

"I think the more logical way to tell this story is that after running Beats for Better and Filter and a bunch of other informal ventures in between, the big lesson that I had is that starting and running a business is really hard. And I think people tend to look at that and think of it as just something that's really obvious but don't think to stop and ask, 'Why?'"

From the Beats for Better venture and several other ventures that followed, Sieo was born to use past experiences to help others start up their own companies. When Kyle and his partners first started the company, the goal was to build a software solution to starting a business, creating an all-in-one tool that allowed clients to enter an idea and take the idea through all of the necessary phases that they needed to go through to become a business. Soon, they realized it needed to be much more specialized and personalized to the companies' needs and Sieo evolved into a startup agency or a startup studio.

They developed a multi-stage process for working with clients:

- Step 1: Validating the business model.
- Step 2: Building a brand and starting to define and shape the product itself.
- Step 3: Building out the strategy behind the business, whether that be marketing or monetization strategies.
- Step 4: Going in and actually building the legal and financial framework for the company to be a startup appropriately set up.

- Step 5: Be an outsourced team member to come on and serve as their design department in their marketing team and their strategy department in their operations team.

"Our vision was that we wanted to provide really high level, almost like Boston Consulting Group or Deloitte level services, at a price point that a startup could afford and do it in such a way that within three months from kicking things off with us, you'd have a fully functional business that was ready to go to market or ready to raise a round of capital."

Kyle, who recently stepped down as CEO to pursue his next venture, shared that although a lot of the success stories are still being written right now, he has a few favorite stories of not just shaping startups but shaping entrepreneurs themselves.

"One of the ones that I love to reference is a company that goes by the name of the Ivy. It's a pretty great story. We met the founder when he was just coming off Wall Street and he had this vision of creating a financial savings application that incentivizes people to pull together and save money for certain goals that they had, whether that be a trip to Cabo or a new car or something like that. What he really saw was a huge issue that is facing Millennials today. And it's not just that they don't save their money, but they don't strategically spend it. And he kind of approached this problem through a technological lens. Not only did he come to us and really build the whole business out with us but also went to the point where he even started to build the product with us and now he's on the App store. And he is up in the thousands of users now. In addition to that, he totally revitalized his life. If you met this guy and found out he's a guy who used to be a straight-faced New Yorker working on Wall Street and now, in his late forties, he acts like a 20-year-old startup founder, you wouldn't believe it."

Kyle explained that for him running an agency was an extremely time-intensive, very exhaustive process, and to do it for two years working day and night with clients took its toll toward burnout.

"I've discovered the biggest and most important thing about entrepreneurship is not your business. That has been a huge reality check for me. In fact, the most important thing about entrepreneurship is you. And if you truly have that balance of body, mind, and soul *are you putting as many hours into your own physical and mental health as you are putting into your business?* And I guarantee you there's no entrepreneur out there who puts as many hours into themselves as they do their business. *Does it feel balanced when you look yourself in the mirror?* I worry that a lot of entrepreneurs end up burning out not because they're working too hard, but because they're not working smart and they're not working on anything else except their business. They're not working on their family relationships. They're not working on their body. They're not working on their mind and not working on their soul. They're not meditating or exercising; they are just working on work. And I have been such a big proponent recently that if you want to have sustained business success, you need to have that balance of body, mind, and soul."

He was looking to find what was next in life, which was to build a really scalable, robust revenue model.

"Sieo was a beautiful business because it so deeply aligned with my personal mission and my personal values, but I think more than anything, it was like boot camp for me. It was a little over two years of just absolute 100 percent, Gary Vee style hustle of 16-hour days every day. And I think I got to a point where I had gone through boot camp, and it was time for me to pursue my next venture. There was this new and very exciting opportunity, which is what I'm doing now, that presented itself to me, which was to work in the blockchain and cryptocurrency space and to work on a business that had a potential for a very, very powerful revenue model to be generated."

Kyle's current company that he co-founded is called Frontier Mining, which he started with a childhood friend, Arland. They were both extremely captivated by cryptocurrency and blockchain trends and Arland had a hardware engineering background he used to build his very own cryptocurrency miner, the hardware infrastructure behind blockchain. It requires really powerful computational abilities to be able to operate and he started to get some demand from within his network for the solution. Kyle promoted it to his network as well and started getting demand right away, and before they knew it, they were in business full-time. The vision for Frontier is to be able to allow people to enter the cryptocurrency market in a more stable way and allow them to diversify their portfolio outside of just purchasing the digital coins themselves.

"The most effective framework for building a business is having people with more experience. And so, with Frontier, what's really allowed us to grow I'd say number one, just me and my partner's shared experience. We have been through a lot. He and I collectively have started, failed, and continued probably six or seven businesses, so we're fairly familiar with what it takes to be an entrepreneur. And then we have really incredible investors who have been ultra-involved and very strategic. And we also have incredible advisors and mentors who have really guided us along a very complex path. When I talked to people about entrepreneurial frameworks, the ones I like to use and which ones have been the most impactful for me, it's 100 percent just been people."

Although Kyle had raised a total of eight figures in investments over his previous ventures, they were having a hard time communicating the value of the new company and raising money. "People look at cryptocurrency the same way they look at porn, where they know that there's a lot of money in it, but they don't really know how the money's made and they don't really want to get their hands on that money," Kyle explained.

Their luck changed when they found a strategic partner while looking at a new facility they could expand their mining operations to. They became close with the head of the demolition company at their target site, telling him how they could help turn the space into a cryptocurrency mining facility generating monthly recurring revenue. Kyle ended up forming a strategic partnership with the demolition company and a real estate investor on the East Coast to find, finance, and launch new cryptocurrency mining facilities.

Kyle emphasized the value of bringing in smart money investors. "I could give a company $10 million, and they could burn through it in a week. That doesn't necessarily guarantee success. Nothing guarantee success. But you've got a better shot if you have someone with experience who is also funding your company, getting involved with your team."

"We have acquired eight facilities right now across the US. We've purchased those, and we're going to slowly convert those into mining facilities or data centers or other high power consuming locations. The partnership worked out great!"

My consulting firm Prepare 4 VC shares a similar mission as Kyle's previous firm Sieo, as a startup itself focused on helping startups. When I formed Prepare 4 VC, LLC in May 2016, I focused on pitch deck presentations and financial projections, leveraging my expertise reviewing hundreds of pitch decks as an investor to help create content for entrepreneurs from the investor's perspective.

I had seen the same trends: 9 out of 10 companies failing, 1.5 percent raising venture funding, and many companies that knew exactly how to pitch their product and sell to customers had no idea how to talk to investors or raise capital. As the organization developed, conversations with current/prospective clients and founders drove the company forward.

Startups had limited budgets pre-funding, so clear, transparent pricing was key. I focused on building package-based solutions instead of hourly projects. Additionally, I found a need for some startup clients who were earlier on in the process to build out a strategy to bootstrap traction that they could then use to be in a better place to fundraise, which led to a new program of weekly strategy sessions to coach and advise founders.

The biggest ask became connections to investors, which were being facilitated through manual introductions to my network at the time. I had an idea to create a platform that would enable accredited investors to have to have access to different alternative investments. My father had syndicated real estate deals for many years and Michael Scanio had extensive real estate analytical and investment experience as well. Both separately managed each deal from scratch and so we came together and created a company whereby we could have an engaged investor community exploring real estate and startup/VC deals.

As we came together and explored opportunities, we saw the value in a platform and investment group approach for accredited investors. We formed a new startup, Equity Venture Partners, as a website and funding platform for accredited investors to learn about and invest in both our real estate deals and the influx of startup deals and angel investment opportunities I was receiving through Prepare 4 VC. We built up a community of investors through monthly webinar events with live pitches from startup founders and our real estate sponsors to fill in the gap and create successful funding opportunities. We have reached a core base of over 180 investors and raised investments of almost $50 million over the first two years since launch.

In 2018, as Equity Venture Partners and Prepare 4 VC grew, I began to search for additional consultants who shared startups helping startups vision to join my projects. I posted on AngelList searching for entrepreneurs and investors to join, on a project basis, leveraging their expertise to help each company.

I received a few inquiries during the first few weeks, and then the applications poured in from hundreds of people who wanted to follow the same *startups helping startups* philosophy. I narrowed it down to the top 50 applicants, bringing eight on board to work on projects and they have all done amazing work.

It was very challenging at first to let go of some of the responsibility and give the project work over to someone else, but I found strengths in each consultant that would offer new value to the client or who could take over project leads in busier months. This has greatly helped our growth.

While we help other startups, it is important to remember we are a startup ourselves and need to live by the values of iteration and listening to customer feedback we preach to clients.

THE GLOBAL COMMUNITY FOR ENTREPRENEURS

In May of 2018, I was chosen to take over the Boston Chapter of StartupGrind, a global community for entrepreneurs founded by Derek Anderson in Silicon Valley and sponsored by Google for Startups. He was a founder himself of technology development group Vaporware labs back in 2010 when Derek started the StartupGrind meetup. His focus at the time was simply to bring in experienced founders and CEOs he could learn from in interviews and fireside chats. He brought in and promoted the events to similar founders to learn from the speakers and quickly the group grew to host major speakers and become one of the most popular startup events in the area. Over the last nine years, StartupGrind has grown rapidly by emulating the model from the original chapter into new cities around the world, spreading to 500 cities across 125 countries that reach a community of two million entrepreneurs.

Each month, every chapter hosts a fireside chat, panel, or networking event to engage the local community and promote entrepreneurship with inspirational stories and lessons from leaders. The group operates under three core values essential to any startup community:

1. We believe in making friends, not contacts.
2. We believe in giving, not taking.
3. We believe in helping others before helping yourself.

It takes a village to raise a startup and no founder can do it alone. Make sure to dedicate time to learning entrepreneurship from others as you grow and scale your business and engage a network that is ready to support you in your endeavors. In the age of entrepreneurship, there are many powerful communities you can join with like-minded founders and entrepreneurs who challenge you to be the best version of yourself.

"What I lack in talent, I compensate with my willingness to grind it out. That's the secret of my life."

—GUY KAWASAKI, MARKETING GURU,

AUTHOR AND VENTURE CAPITALIST

**

VENTURING FORWARD TAKEAWAYS:

- Failure is expected, but using other people's failures to breed success is ideal.
- Always expect the unexpected and be set up to adapt.
- Living a balanced lifestyle is key to avoiding burnout and keeping the same passion for your work that you start with on day one.

THE PIVOT

"A founder's skill is knowing how to recognize new patterns and pivot on a dime"

—STEVE BLANK, THE FATHER OF
MODERN ENTREPRENEURSHIP.

It is official: Amazon is buying Twitch.

Amazon announced that it is spending nearly a billion dollars to buy the game-streaming service Twitch.

Amazon stepped in. They wanted the flow, they wanted the audience.

As it turns out, a stunning 1.35 percent of all internet traffic is devoted to nothing but watching people play video games.

The CEO of Twitch, Emmett Shear, wrote in a statement, "We chose Amazon because they believe in our community, they share our values and long-term vision, and they want to help us get there faster.[22]"

In 2014, Amazon acquired a streaming platform called Twitch where gamers live-stream themselves playing video games and viewers around the world tune in to watch. The startup was a major success, but it did not start out that way.

Before Twitch was Twitch, it was a 24-7 live stream of co-founder Justin Kan's seemingly average life at the time. Just like many success stories, it took a major pivot to get to where the company is today. Constant innovation and listening to customer wants and needs can turn average ideas into incredible companies.

PHOTO-SHARING PHENOMENON

Before Instagram was Instagram, it was a small platform called Burbn named after the founder's favorite beverage. In 2010, Kevin Systrom marveled at the success of check-in

---

22 "Twitch 2: Gaming the System." Gimlet. Gimlet. April 22, 2016.

applications like Foursquare but believed there was one key aspect they were not capitalizing on: the phone camera. Kevin was a very competent and fast coder, putting together a complex application of check-in and social media features within the first three months for a beta release[23].

"It was just compelling enough to get a handful of beta users, but I would basically come home at night and just tinker with this idea. And along the way, I prototyped it enough that I was willing to give it to a handful of friends," Kevin explains in an interview on NPR's *How I Built This* with Guy Raz.

"Those friends gave it to a handful of friends and before you knew it, we had—I don't know—maybe 80, 90 people using it. Only at that moment did I decide that maybe this thing could be a company if we actually tried. I went to a bar where a bunch of investors were getting together and mingled around the room, and people were showing their prototypes on their phones to different investors. I showed it to this one investor, named Steve Anderson. He was one of our first investors. He was impressed and said, 'This is pretty cool. Let's set up coffee. We can meet up and you can tell me more about the app.' And that was the biggest accomplishment to date. I remember thinking, 'Oh, my God, there's an investor who's willing to talk to us.'

23 Garber, Megan. 2014a. "None." The Atlantic. The Atlantic. July 2, 2014.

"So I went, and I had that coffee. I sat down and I had an alert set on my phone that would go off every time someone signed up because I was really excited when we went from 80 users to 85 users to 90 users. And as I'm sitting there with him, a bunch of people were signing up. I wasn't entirely sure why, but he looked at me and said, 'Did you plan this so you would have a bunch of people sign up while you were demoing to me?' And I said, 'No, I honestly don't know who these people are,' and he looks at me and says, 'All right, count me in.' But he actually said one thing to me, too. He goes, 'Before I do this, you have to find a co-founder that's willing to do this with you.' At that moment, I thought, 'All right, I have got to find someone awesome to partner with and make this all happen.'"

Michael Kreiger was a developer, tinkerer, and entrepreneur like Kevin who worked out of the same San Francisco coffee shop, Coffee Bar. They connected over the application and a shared vision, with Michael and Kevin ultimately joining forces on the project. At the time, there were a little over a hundred users, two team members, and interest from two Silicon Valley investors that were ready to commit what would become a combined $500K in capital into the business.

"No one wants to miss the next Google, the next whatever. And that initial check went from $50,000 to $250,000. And then there was another investor, Andreessen Horowitz, who came in and put $250,000 in. So here are two guys with basically a prototype and a couple of computers, no office, who raised a half a million dollars. And we're looking at each other thinking, 'We think we can make this last.' I mean, we were living on peanut butter and jelly sandwiches at the time," Kevin explains on *How I Built This*.

The podcast host, Guy Raz, prodded his story along, "So how did you guys pivot? I mean, how did you turn Burbn into what became Instagram? What was the genesis of that?"

Kevin said, "I think the best thing for any entrepreneur is failure. And for us, it was the lack of momentum. I mentioned we got to about 100 users using this app."

"A hundred, not 100,000, a hundred?" Guy clarified. The big success that would later became Instagram struggled to get past its hundredth user.

"No, no, no, a hundred. You could fit them in a room. And Eric Ries is this guy in Silicon Valley who likes to talk about the lean startup method. One of his lines is, 'Don't ask why people don't use your startup. Ask why the people who continue to use your startup keep using it.' And when we looked at our user base, our whole hundred people, each of them loved the photo aspect. So that's why we ended up focusing on photos," Kevin explains.

Burbn would pivot to find its core feature: photo-sharing. Kevin and Michael figured out their batch of an initial 100 users stuck with it because of the photo-sharing element and made this the driving force of the application. However, they also knew that photo-sharing was an increasingly popular space, and they had to identify a unique competitive advantage in the new direction of the application.

During the pivot, Michael and Kevin felt discouraged over the lack of growth and the obstacles in creating a powerful photo-sharing application everyone would use. The two agreed to alternate breaks to clear their heads. Michael would prototype some of the initial ideas while Kevin took a break on a short vacation with his wife to Mexico. It was on this trip, discussing the application with his wife, in which the big breakthrough occurred.

"As I'm away, I'm walking down the beach with Nicole in Mexico. We were in this little surfing town called Todos Santos and I said, 'You know, Nicole, I think we're going to focus on photos.'" Kevin explained to Guy how his wife helped him come up with the idea to add filters to the app while lamenting that her photos never look as good as their friends' photos.

Kevin immediately went back to the hacienda after their walk on the beach and began researching how to create the perfect filter, what would become Xx-Pro. The goal and vision was clear now, the platform would allow everyday people to create and share photos that looked professionally photographed.

Michael and Kevin coded the application and had it up in the in the App Store within eight weeks, launching under the new brand Instagram. Within 24 hours of launch, the app went viral with 25,000 signups. The application was not without its glitches, constantly crashing the Instagram servers as the user base scaled with negative feedback on Twitter about 'Yet another startup that doesn't know how to scale.'

Kevin, Michael, and a team of 11 pulled the startup together to scale globally over the first two years, rapidly expanding every time a major celebrity from Snoop Dogg to President Obama and Justin Bieber joined the site. The biggest pride and joy of the founders was seeing what they built in action everywhere they turned, knowing they created something people use and love.

By 2012, Facebook had made an offer to acquire the firm. Instagram sold for a $1 billion valuation.

"The first day that we went home after pulling that all-nighter to launch Instagram, there was a guy sitting on the Muni here in San Francisco, which is the subway system, and he was using Instagram. And I remember thinking, 'Oh, my god, we did it! Someone in the world is using this thing out in the wild," Kevin recalls. "That feeling in that moment is the currency that you maximize when you're an entrepreneur. Seeing someone using your product and loving it is way more rewarding than any amount of money in the world[24]."

TWITCHING WITH SUCCESS

"When Emmett called me and told me what the latest price that he had negotiated was, I was actually in a conference room somewhere else, and I dropped down on my knees and was just laughing my ass off. I cannot believe that. We built a company, and it's worth a *billion* dollars? That's pretty amazing. And we were all at Kyle's wedding the day the actual wires hit our bank, and I remember opening up my Bank of America app and thinking, I didn't even know you could put that much money in Bank of America. You know, all the co-founders were there, and we just thought it was incredible," recalled Twitch co-founder Justin Kan on an episode of Gimlet Media's podcast *Startup*

Nine months before the Amazon sale, Justin was trying to sell some of his shares to investors in the private market around the $200 million price tag. Every single investor had turned him down.

---

24 "NPR Choice Page." 2019. Npr.Org. 2019.

When Twitch was launched in 2007, it was a completely different platform from the video game streaming giant Twitch became. Originally called Justin.TV, the company started as the internet's first reality TV show with an entertainment platform built around the show. Co-founder Justin Kan clipped a camera to his hat live-streaming his life 24/7 on the platform while his team worked behind the scenes, running the website and the business.

"People would come to the site and then very quickly, they'd say, 'This is the most boring thing I've ever seen,' and they'd just leave; 99 percent of them would just close it," Justin said.

But some users kept coming back with the same question, **"How do I create my own video stream?"** They wanted to be stars of their own live streaming shows, which led to the first pivot of the platform, a service to allow anyone to live stream content and became an internet star. Investors loved the new idea and co-founder Michael Seibel raised $2 million to kick-start the new platform.

"So after this pivot, with their new investment money, Justin and his co-founders moved into their first real office. They hired some employees and then, in October 2007, they officially relaunched as the YouTube of live video," Lisa Chow of Gimlet media explains on the podcast *Startup*. "There wasn't as much press this time, but there were a lot more users. That first week, more than half a million people visited the site. They live-streamed their pets or themselves sitting at home at their computer, playing video games. Occasionally, you'd catch couples arguing or silly dares between friends. But with more people came more problems. The site broke all the time. Bandwidth costs were out of control. And the same things happening today were happening back then. Men harassed women with gross sexual comments. People live-streamed horrible things. One person live-streamed his suicide. Justin and his team could not control what was happening on the site."

By 2009, the biggest issue on their platform was concerns over piracy. Users would point their cameras at the TV to live stream entire sporting events, bypassing the cable networks and copyright laws. The company was summoned to Washington DC where CEO Michael Seibel testified at the hearing.

"That morning, I remember I felt horrible. I didn't want to get out of bed. I was watching it on C-SPAN, while I was lying there, thinking, 'Oh, my god, this is awful,'" Justin said. "We were the scapegoat for internet piracy, even though we were completely compliant with the law. And also cooperating above and beyond it. So it was more of a negative PR cluster bomb dropped on our head and we thought it was completely unjust but also made us look completely toxic."

No rulings were set against the company, but the press and negative publicity caused major setbacks in the company timeline. The growth was slow, and they were struggling to raise additional capital, so they made a second major pivot in the business model, focusing on profitability. The management team made a list of all the places that they could make money with extra ad units around the site, auto-playing video ads on content and cutting costs by laying off employees and renegotiating terms with suppliers. And within three months, they would break even and become profitable shortly after.

"I can't explain to you how this is the moment where everyone dies. And, we didn't just not die, we home-runned it. And so, we were actually pretty proud of ourselves, to be completely honest," Michael Seibel, the CEO explains.

The team was re-energized and excited about the profitable technology business they had built, until a meeting with a prominent industry veteran, who had worked in the top ranks at Facebook and YouTube, brought them back down to earth.

"He came over to the office, and we were talking about how we were proud. And he said, 'Everything you've done so far is insignificant. Within three years, you'll be forgotten, and the money that you're making now is going to go away. You've done nothing.' We realized that we *had* done nothing. We realized that we weren't going to be able to raise more money, we weren't going to be able to build more demand. There weren't going to be acquirers. This was kind of a dead-end for working on that product," said Michael.

The team had hit on one of the fundamentals behind the technology revolution: profitability was great for keeping the lights on or building a sustainable business, but if they wanted to be acquired, they would have to focus on growth. Companies buy other technologies for many reasons, the complexity of the software itself, the revenue they can bring in house and turn profitable through economies of scale, the user base they can leverage for other product lines, or the team they can bring under a similar mission, but all areas were rooted around the same goal of showing powerful growth to a potential acquirer.

Over the next few months, CTO Emmett focused on taking a step back to think about how he used the platform. He was an avid gamer and spent most of his time on the platform watching professionals and semi-pros play video games. Digging into the data, he found that only 2 percent of the userbase focused on gaming, but they were extremely passionate and active users. The team focused on interviewing gamers on the platform to find out why they streamed and how the team could make their experience better with new features or updates. Every gamer they talked to validated the opportunity and the company transitioned to its final pivot, a streaming platform for gamers called Twitch. This new-found focus led to explosive growth as the company found its community. It reached 55 million active users watching over 15 billion minutes of content by the time Amazon purchased the company in 2014 in a $1 billion acquisition.

**

Researching and discovering successful pivots was a driving force behind the creation of EQx Fund launched in January 2018 by my partner, Ziad Moukheiber, and I. The idea behind the fund is simple: startups change and ideas pivot along the way, but the constant that remains to drive the company to succeed is the entrepreneur. The fund is focused on the founders and their ability to lead a team, spot opportunities to pivot, and bring the company to success.

Where IQ is a representation of a person's intelligence, we put the focus on EQ or Emotional Quotient. This includes leadership qualities that are essential to being an entrepreneur and the ability to find and bring in those with highly relevant IQs onto their team. The founder does not necessarily have to be the smartest person in the room on every subject: They should know who that person is and when to turn to them for feedback as a leader.

We take a unique approach in considering our portfolio of founders, rather than our portfolio of startups, with a very successful group of entrepreneurs to date. Out of our first 13 investments to date, five have had previous large scale acquisitions or IPOs of last ventures, a few have given up leading corporate positions at companies Pfizer and Google to pursue their passions, and the rest have proven their leadership qualities through our ongoing interactions and their ability to bring on impressive teammates, customers, advisors, investors, and board members that they actively listen to in order to move the company forward.

One portfolio company HealthTech Solutions underwent a pivot to become OmniLife.ai, focusing on the Artificial Intelligence component of their transplant center application and the ability to save lives through automated matching and real-time, HIPAA compliant chat between organ transplant centers to place organs with patients in need.

Another portfolio company, Tunnel, has made a minor pivot as well in the blockchain space to focus on institutional B2B transactions between banks when they received overwhelming interest on the corporate side while they were working on compliance for a public cryptocurrency model of their technology. The system is a patented multi-chain solution that is faster and cheaper than current blockchain architectures and a small-scale pivot has allowed the company to accelerate its growth and revenue timeline. We expect many of our startups to change or find new niches along the way, and the leaders will make all of the difference.

FAILURE BREEDS SUCCESS

Before Slack was a member of the Unicorn Club at a $7 billion+ valuation for its corporate messaging and chat application, the company started as a video game production firm called Tiny Peck, gaining fame on their interactive game called Glitch. The point of Glitch was that there *was* no point: unlike traditional video games with a clear start and end, users of Glitch would play in a virtual setting with an endless goal. Founder Stewart Butterfield described the game as "Monty Python crossed with Dr. Seuss on acid[25]."

Players could interact with each other, collect resources, personalize their avatars, and use their resources to create homes—an early version of the popular game Minecraft. Although users seemed to be addicted to the game, they were becoming more and more addicted to their iPhones and Apple products, and as a Flash Player game at the time, most users were ditching non-compatible games in favor of Game Apps. Glitch shut down in 2012 and Tiny Peck dug

---

25   https://www.fastcompany.com/3026418/this-story-about-slacks-founder-says-everything-you-need-to-know-about-him

into their successes and failures to figure out what was next for the company[26].

In building the game Glitch, the developers had needed constant communication, updates, file sharing, and messaging in a way that wasn't available on any of the other standard messaging dashboards, so they had built their own internal messaging platform for the developers at Tiny Speck. After dwindling the team to its core, making sure they found jobs elsewhere for every team member they let go, Stewart and the team set out to build on the messaging concept and test its applications in the corporate world, calling the company Slack.

The new pivot was a huge success. From pure word of mouth through Beta site referrals and reviews, Slack quickly grew from an internal project to 16,000 users and beyond. On February 2014, leading VC and investor in what was now Slack, Marc Andreessen tweeted: "I have never seen a viral enterprise app take off like this before— all word of mouth.[27]"

---

26 Hartigan, Matt. 2014. "This Story About Slack's Founder Says Everything You Need To Know About Him." Fast Company. Fast Company. February 12, 2014.

27 "Becoming Slack: The Story of a Son of a Glitch — SitePoint." 2016. SitePoint. February 5, 2016.

As of May 2019, the company had filed for IPO and was preparing to go public not for capital needs but as a chance to let investors and employees cash out on the company's success to date. The last investment round placed a valuation of over 7 billion dollars on the business chat application that started as a mere feature of the video game Glitch. This is not Stewart's first failed video game turned successful technology platform either. His previous startup before Glitch spawned out of features that he developed for an earlier video game involving photo sharing, which ended up becoming the platform Flickr.

His lesson: Focus on what works in the products you develop and each simple success can become a platform of its own.

PINNING DOWN THE CUSTOMER

In 2009, Ben Silbermann and his cofounders Paul Sciarra and Vikram Bhaskaran set out on a mission to change the face of the consumer shopping experience with their application Tote. Tote plugged into retail chains like Banana Republic, Anthropologie, and American Eagle, allowing users to save their favorite items to get alerts when the clothing went on sale. The company quickly gained interest, winning the NYU Stern business plan competition and finding their first lead investor in Brian Cohen, chairman of the New York Angels.

"I don't really care what you're doing, I'll invest with you," Brian told Ben after hearing his 15-second elevator pitch on the product. Ben had nailed the customer problem so well right away that Brian not only was ready to invest, but he also became a power user, unsubscribing from all of the retail catalogs he received and going digital on Tote. While Tote had found a real problem and growing userbase, the initial vision of the company was not panning out as the team had hoped. Between a suboptimal online payment system and a lack of trust in mobile payments at the time, transactions and conversions among users into purchasers were extremely low. However, there was one feature that everyone seemed to use. People would take the collections of saved items and share them with their friends.

When Ben and his team came back to Brian and the other investors to share the pivot of the company into a new direction and brand of Pinterest, Brian was fully on board and reinvested in the new round. He viewed the pivot as a positive realization of the customer and a step forward for the company: "It was a direct outgrowth of what he learned from the first business. Ben saw an unmet need, and obviously a huge opportunity[28]." The new bet paid off, as Pinterest is

---

28   Cale Guthrie Weissman. 2019. "A 360-Degree Tour of Specialized Bicycles' Innovation Lab." Fast Company. Fast Company. May 17, 2019.

now a public company with a market capitalization of $13.97 billion as of May 2019.

**

Just as Pinterest came out of Tote, Twitch launched from Justin.TV, Glitch became Slack, and Instagram developed from Burbn, many startups also spawn out of experiences founders encountered in their previous ventures. Instead of a pivot, a successful brand and exit can lead to a second successful brand as an offshoot of the first. We have several investments through the EQx Fund so far in founders that we hope will follow this model.

David Friend, the founder of data storage giant Carbonite (NASDAQ: CARB), found an unmet need in the cloud storage space with his new venture Wasabi. Todd Zion who had previously sold Smart Cells to Merck in a $500 million exit in the diabetes space founded a new venture and application in insulin engineering in Akston Biosciences. And Tom Schultz has taken the difficult pathway of developing a successful worldwide approved drug that treats and eliminates diarrhea in humans and his new company Anubis has a product Doggy Stat that eliminates the issue in the pet industry and treats diseases like Parvo. Whether it is a pivot, a rebrand, or a launch of a new venture, it is important to learn from past experiences and leverage the expertise you have gained from your most valuable resource: the customer.

"I've missed more than 9,000 shots in my career. I've lost almost 300 games. 26 times I've been trusted to take the game-winning shot and missed. I've failed over and over and over again in my life and that is why I succeed."

—MICHAEL JORDAN, NBA LEGENDARY BASKETBALL MVP

**

- Watch who uses your platform and how to focus on the most important features. Successful startups have simple concepts they execute well.
- It is okay to take a step back, a walk on the beach and think. Some of the best ideas come outside of the office.
- Bet on the jockey, not the horse. A great entrepreneur can find new directions and pivots for the company that may not have even been part of the original concept.

THE PITCH

—

"I think what I provide is a forum and a window into technology. So if I'm entertained by it or if this is very interesting to me and I like it, that's a way in the door. You may or may not raise money, but you have to have a story that's interesting and you have to tell it well"

—MIC WILLIAMS, FOUNDER OF BOSTON HARBOR ANGELS

"Okay, let's take a walk and give me your pitch," an investor asked.

"Okay, here is the problem: in the world of audio right now most people consume, in the kind of audio journalism that I do, most people consume it over the radio. Those people are leaving the radio in droves and they're migrating to digital. They're migrating to digital listening. The number of, obviously smartphone handsets are going through the roof, the audio dashboard is becoming digital, the iTunes radio, podcasting is all gonna be on your dashboard, and there's this whole world of… all these people going there and I want to start a company that will create the content for all these people to listen to who are moving into the digital future slash present."

As he plays the recording of his first big investor pitch to the listeners of *Startup: The Podcast,* Alex Blumberg is definitely disappointed with the way he pitched[29].

Alex was a famous radio journalist of *This American Life* and *Planet Money,* yet he struggled with the pitch. And this was not just any investor who asked him to take a walk and make a pitch.

It was billionaire investor, Chris Sacca, who had invested early into Twitter and was one of the largest shareholders when it went public.

To follow on from there, Chris pitched back to Alex how he would have done the 30-second elevator pitch with all

---

29 Baribeau, Simone. 2012. "The Pinterest Pivot." Fast Company. Fast Company. October 23, 2012.

the pros for investing, as well as another quick pitch against investing in this type of business.

Pitching is hard even for professional speakers. Fundraising is hard, only 1.5 percent of startup businesses ever get any sort of venture capital financing.

But if you can tell your story, build a relationship, and get investors on board, the power to build a brand and expand is incredible.

THE BIG CHECK

"I've always liked helping people, and I've always liked technology. Growing up, I was always doing kind of business-y-things but never called it entrepreneurship," Adam Sobol, serial entrepreneur and current founder of Care-Band, recalls in our interview. "In high school, I went to an entrepreneurship competition and a few hackathons and I even started a video-making business, making videos and websites for different people and organizations around my community. And then in college, I started a company during my sophomore year with two of my fraternity brothers: I went to Indiana University, and we saw a need for selling student-to-student tickets, so like a StubHub for student tickets."

Indiana University is a huge basketball school and grabbing a student ticket to the games was highly competitive. Students could sell tickets and make a good amount of money, but they could only sell their student section tickets to either their friends on campus through word of mouth or by using Facebook or Craigslist. Instead, Adam and his co-founder created a platform called UniversityTix.com that connected people to be able to sell tickets.

"That was my first real point into entrepreneurship and I realized that I really, *really* liked building things. I saw an opportunity to make money with it, which was just awesome. Then from there, started another company after that in college and then started here at CareBand after that," Adam explained. Adam was in a Cybersecurity program, so in school, he had learned high-level coding and web development to tie the project together with an app and website for the student-to-student transactions.

"The ability to sit at a computer and build something in a matter of hours and then make money off of it is a crazy experience. And the ability to push the envelope as far as you can, until you break something, is really exciting. And then see the results of whatever you do instantly." Adam and his team bought branded stickers for UniversityTix.com and placed them all around campus, which was a huge success and brought an influx of users on board, until they got a letter from the city saying they had to stop or face significant fines. The guerrilla marketing approaches continued as they tried every trick to grow recognition and usage around campus.

"During the first few years, the transactions were terrible. But then we got better and better at it and we were able to update the website and make it more user-friendly. And at the end, we had about 5,000 people using the site, 5,000 students and we made a few thousand dollars. So it was a great, great first starting point," Adam recalled. As team members graduated, Adam and his partner ended up selling the application to another group of students to take over. He had achieved his first small exit and gained the skills and experience for his next venture.

In developing Adam's current company, he leveraged ideas he had seen at his father's geriatric practice, taking from his own startup experience to develop the CareBand device and software for location and activity monitoring in senior care facilities. His father manages 10,000 seniors living in Ohio and growing up, Adam would always visit the nursing homes with him.

"I would always go to the nursing home with him and look around and all the technology was ancient or there really wasn't very much technology at all. So, I figured there was a need in the market and about four years ago when Apple released new technology called 'beacon technology,' I saw a ton of potential for how this technology could help."

Beacons are devices designed to send data on low power Bluetooth to different connected devices and it enabled a wave of new applications. Adam's vision was to use this new technology to help seniors living with dementia who wander and get lost, and after market exploration, there was limited competition. He decided to launch CareBand to solve the mission he had set out on.

"So, it's a long, *long* journey, but I started a company about four years ago. And initially it was just bootstrapped from me trying to do as much as I could and then we realized we needed some more significant funding and validation. So after building a few prototypes, we won a startup weekend in Bloomington, Indiana and we didn't win any funding then, but they wrote about us in the paper and our message started to get out," Adam recalls. "And then after that, we applied for this other competition that Indiana called The BEST competition. It stands for Building Entrepreneurs in Software and Technology. That competition was basically anybody could apply and then they picked 10 finalists and then only two companies to invest in, and they invest $100,000 in you. And the money is made up of about 20 really famous Indiana University alumni, so it's not just the university giving you money, but it is real money from entrepreneurs and really famous people around from the university. So anyway, I applied for that and I made it to the finals the first year I entered but I didn't end up winning. I kept working on it the year after, applied again, and CareBand ended up winning! So I won $100,000. It is crazy, you know. It is a crazy thing as a college student to have $100,000 in your bank account."

Adam harnessed the true MVP power discussed earlier in this book to win these competitions and build momentum. His initial prototype wasn't a hardware device but rather two iPhones coded so that when the patient phone became far enough away from the caregiver phone, the caregiver would receive an alert message. Many people think of competitions as just the prize money or just the marketing exposure, but as Adam's story unfolded, it became much more than that.

"It was just kind of a crazy experience. One of the investors from the $100,000 competition was very impressed with what we had done so far with the company and wanted to keep supporting us," Adam explained. "So after some conversations that were more like mentorship conversations, he said, 'I'm going to be in Chicago, you should come down to my hotel.' So I went over and then he whips out a check for $50,000 and just handed to me in his nice fancy hotel. And I walked out thinking $100,000 was a lot but that went straight into the bank account. But holding a piece of paper that's worth $50,000 is just a crazy experience."

CareBand finished the final prototypes and devices in January 2019 and started piloting them at a few different nursing homes in Chicago and in Indiana with positive feedback as they go into the full production phase.

"We have such an opportunity and there's not a lot of technology still that is out there for this population. And our world is aging, as you might know. It's our turn as young people to help and to build things that are valuable." Adam is on a powerful mission to change the world, and the momentum kicked off with a pitch at a business plan competition.

**

"A pitch is done when you are done taking information out of it."
—ZIAD MOUKHEIBER, EQX FUND AND
BOSTON HARBOR ANGELS

"It grinds my gears when founders paint a completely perfect picture and aren't willing to open up with the challenges they've had to overcome and are still facing. It's very easy to

spot someone who is dancing around a direct question. Noth-
ing is ever perfectly up and to the right, and that's okay! We
want to have an open and honest discussion, and that's how
we can be helpful!"

—ROB MCCALL, .406 VENTURES

"It frosts me when entrepreneurs tell me how much time and
money have been spent getting to where they are today in the
hopes of supporting a higher company 'valuation.' I frankly
don't care if you've spent years and millions building some-
thing that's worth only a dime. To ask us to give you more than
a dime for it is nonsense. You need to look at what you've built
and what its potential is and price it accordingly. We don't buy
past expenditures, we buy the future."

—BEN LITTAUER, WALNUT VENTURES

"You know what really grinds my gears? As is cogently
expressed by Michael Mark in Episode 1 there is always
the temptation to pursue more than one opportunity at
a time. Given the minimal resources startups command,
they need to hone in on the activity that gives them the best
chance of success. However, founders should avoid being
so single-minded that they persist on a failed business
plan too long. You will note that this is a recurring theme
on all the podcasts because achieving the right balance

between these two is really hard and founders agonize about it frequently."

—SAL DAHER, PODCAST HOST OF ANGEL INVEST BOSTON

I make it a mission of mine as I coach startups through the fundraising process with Prepare 4 VC and constantly meet founders and listen to pitches for EQx Fund to discuss with other investors what *grinds their gears* in a startup pitch. Pitching is hard and everyone has pet peeves to avoid in the pitch. Connecting with the investors and learning from them, getting feedback and advice can make all the difference.

On the other side, when investors are asked what they do like to see in a pitch, the response is almost unanimous: **We like to hear a story.**

The startup story emphasizes three parts—a beginning, middle, and end:

1. In the beginning, there was a huge problem faced by the industry. It affects millions of lives worldwide, and there is a reason no one else has come up with a solution before.
2. In the middle, the startup came up with a novel innovation to solve the problem. They proved the market with certain traction points or customer feedback, or have a clear plan and milestones laid out to do so.

And in the end, the trickiest part, the company meets its goal of scaling rapidly and getting acquired, going public, etc. This becomes the tricky part because it needs to be believable. The startup will be acquired because they have an amazing team that can do it better than anyone else, the technology itself is incredible, or the customer base and data they are gathering are so valuable to any other company looking to enter this space.

Simply telling a great startup story and projecting it to investors can turn your pitch from an ask to an opportunity.

**

After professional storyteller and radio journalist Alex Blumberg had his pitch for his new podcasting company shot down, reworked, and pitched back to him by Chris Sacca, Chris gave him an opportunity to try again. He set up an introduction to his business partner, Matt Mazzeo, and told Alex that if he could convince Matt to jump on board, he would follow.

"I spent the last week or so gathering advice on how to make my pitch better. I focused it on a personal story at the beginning to establish rapport. I've made the opportunity seem bigger. As a friend told me, no one wants to hear about Odysseus going to the corner store. Investors are like everyone else… they want to be part of something large. So I've added some impressive-sounding numbers like 240 million radio listeners that account for an average of 12 to 13 hours a week and they are inevitably going to transition to digital, on-demand listening. And also I'd given my company a name, *The American Podcasting Corporation.* And what we are going to do is we are going to connect audiences to digital programming that they want to listen to."

Alex met Matt in the lobby of a hotel and had his pitch perfected this time. He had all of the answers lined up and projected figures in his mind that he believed would be achievable and would be a huge success in his mind if everything came together as planned.

"I'm definitely going to spend more time with you. Normally I would say if I wasn't interested and I'd give you three reasons why," Matt told Alex at the end of his pitch. "But I can tell you this one is interesting enough to me because I don't think there are too many people with your pedigree willing to take a leap into entrepreneurship, and you have the opportunity and the access to build brand as quickly effectively. I think you proved that you have an eye for content, which is in my mind really, really hard today. And so this fits a bunch of the things that we look for in a business, which includes an entrepreneur who is audacious and also probably the best at what they're going to go out and build. Yes, it is worthy of spending more time."

Matt was ready to dive in and continue the diligence process, but to Alex's surprise, where he had expected pushback on the achievability of his goals laid out, Matt wanted more. He thought Alex was underestimating the potential market for podcast listeners and did not project out fast enough scalability with only three new shows per year. Matt also pushed Alex to consider the opportunity for a technology platform in the space instead of becoming the content provider.

Alex describes the process, "I gave the best picture I could give, the biggest dream I could dream, and the answer was still, 'Yes, but how does it scale?' There's a point in the interview where Matt asked me, 'Okay, so a couple years from now, you have got a big marketing department and a huge sales force. How are you going to expand your listener base?' Not only could I not answer the question, I really couldn't accept the premise."

Alex highlights one of the main decisions and roadblocks in an early-stage company: to go the venture route or to go what is called the lifestyle business route. Neither way is right nor wrong, but the vision of the parties involved have to be aligned. A venture-funded company has the goal of growth: don't become a podcasting company, become *the* podcasting company, producing as many shows, features, or technology to as many users as quickly as possible raising capital to support growth.

Venture Capital funds make money for their investors by having equity in companies that exit: an investor buys shares early on and either another company, a private equity firm, or public market investors from an IPO buy those shares for a significant return on investment at a later date. The lifestyle company, on the other hand, is focused on sustainable growth: put a small team together to build out a few podcasts and leverage the advertising profits or debt opportunities to expand and grow the company and audience from there. There are examples of very successful businesses going both routes, but Alex needed to choose the best path for him.

Ultimately, Alex decided that he was ready to go all-in and aim to become a podcasting giant. He found a co-founder, branded his new company Gimlet, and raised investment from Chris, Matt, and several other investors to hit the ground running. Season 1 of *Startup: The Podcast* chronicles Alex's journey and reminds us all that building a startup is not an easy task, but it can be a very rewarding one[30]. After several years of hard work and sleepless nights, Gimlet Media was purchased by Spotify in February 2019. The purchase price: $230 million for the company Alex doubted could be big enough to hit his projections[31]. $230 million for the

30 StartUp. 2014a. "Gimlet 1: How Not to Pitch a Billionaire." Gimlet. Gimlet. April 6, 2014.

31 StartUp. 2014b. "Gimlet 2: Is Podcasting the Future or the Past?" Gimlet. Gimlet. September 5, 2014.

startup that stumbled in its first pitch and then turned into a story and a pitch that live on in history.

SHAPING YOUR STORY

Throughout this book, you have heard stories from founders across the United States with a variety of backgrounds, products, services, and paths they have taken to venture forward. Every startup story is unique and can be built upon the lessons and innovative practices of previous companies. When pitching to investors, customers, or partners, it becomes essential to highlight your story and pull out the most important components that will get the listener excited about what you are doing. Know your audience and what they are looking for.

When you pitch an investor, remember that this is their job, and they have heard hundreds or thousands of pitches in their lifetime. They may have heard, invested in, or even built companies that are similar to yours and are looking for you to answer one simple question: *Why should I invest in your company instead of the other startups in my pipeline?* The pitch needs to be presented not as a request for money but as an opportunity to buy equity in the next hot startup.

Investors have various portfolio strategies, interests, and backgrounds that make up their decisions, and it is important to find a group that shares the same vision as your company.

Does your investor hope you can build a company that can scale and be sold with a limited amount of capital?

Do they want you to shoot for a home run opportunity, raising large amounts and scaling as aggressively as possible?

Are they a strategic partner or impact investor that is just as focused on bringing the technology into the world as they are on creating a return?

Does your investor want to be involved in the day to day life of your company or take a hands-off approach?

The only wrong answer here is not knowing the answer and having founders, board members, and investors being on different pages. While the investors interview you for their portfolio, interview them for your capitalization table (list of equity holders). This will become one of the most important relationships of the startup life, a marriage and commitment between the startup and its investors. Find your perfect match and venture forward.

**

"Investors are not solely evaluating your company's story. They are also evaluating your ability to convey that story" —Bill Gurley, General Partner at Benchmark

VENTURING FORWARD TAKEAWAYS

- The most important part of a pitch is the story you tell.
- View every encounter with investors as a chance to build relationships, even a pitch contest may turn into an opportunity much bigger than you expected.
- Not every investor is right for every company. Do your diligence on them as well while they evaluate your company.

CONCLUSION

"The only way to win is to learn faster than anyone else."

—ERIC RIES, AUTHOR OF *THE LEAN STARTUP*

"You can't polish a turd.

"You can have a bad idea, and you can spend years trying to polish it and it just doesn't work. So what I do is that I launch a lot of ideas sometimes in parallel and then the good ideas instantly stand out. And then you just go pursue the good," said Alex Mehr, the founder of online dating giant Zoosk and current founder and CEO of Mentorbox[32]. Alex has launched 30 different products throughout his career, many in parallel,

---

32   "ALEX MEHR: LAUNCHING BUSINESSES AND SUCCEEDING IN THE USA." 2019. YouTube Video. *YouTube.*

testing the market to find the opportunities that turn into companies. His current venture, EQx Fund portfolio company MentorBox, is a subscription service promoted as the *Netflix for Books*, a service to receive monthly curated books and a platform for online video interviews and workshops with authors, CEOs, and investors.

MentorBox's thesis: The average CEO reads 60 books per year for their constant learning—for their 10 percent better every day. The average person does not have the time or expertise to find what to read or who to learn from, and MentorBox helps bridge the gap. As I join the world of authors, I hope this book served as an outlet for lessons from a variety of leaders that you can bring into your entrepreneurial journey.

Alex has featured guests like Arianna Huffington, of the *Huffington Post*, Patrick Lee of *Rotten Tomatoes*, and many more inspirational leaders on the MentorBox platform. His secret to connecting and getting in touch with these mentors and advisors: *Do not try to sell the first time.* "I'm a very non-salesy person. I try to give value before I even ask for anything and I do that many times and I honestly don't expect anything in return. So what I do is that I just tried to give, and I have a friend of mine, Patrick Lee, a good friend of mine and he actually shot a whole course on networking for MentorBox. He's the founder and former CEO of *Rotten Tomatoes*. He is a super networker and his advice is exactly that. He basically gives and gives and gives and expects nothing in return but it always comes back."

As you think about the pathway through this book, reflect on the topics you have learned as well as those you realize that you want to learn more about. Seek knowledge, seek leadership and guidance, and someday you will become a leader yourself.

**

Every startup is a journey and while no two startup stories are identical, you are not alone in your journey. Hundreds or thousands of entrepreneurs have been in a similar position to you at every stage of your venture. For every challenge you face, there is a story you can learn from as you grow your own business.

There is no right way to find a startup idea. It can come from a personal problem like FutureFuel, an issue in business like Brex, an opportunity you see in the world like Noticare, or even completely by accident—a solution looking for its problem to solve like the case of Silly Putty.

Startups do not have to fit into a stereotypical mold. We have heard stories from male and female founders, American and International entrepreneurs, technology founders, consumer product and wine companies, healthcare and aerospace applications. We have seen companies that started as a gaming company turn into a business chat application as in the case of Slack, and numerous examples of serial entrepreneurs taking small successes or failures to build something huge the next time around.

As you go through your own startup journey, writing your own startup tale, I hope you look back on the lessons of the entrepreneurs in this book and channel their inspiration to help you forward. I hope this book fosters your entrepreneurial spirit and helps you take the leap toward whatever goals you have for you and your company. As we watch the startup community and culture continue to grow, help the entrepreneurs around you and share your own wisdom with others. Every little tip, trick, story, or piece of advice can make all of the difference. My hope for all of my readers is that their startup and their story makes it into my next book, sharing and inspiring a wave of new entrepreneurs to follow in their path.

How will your story unfold? Only time will tell, but as a reader seeking out advice and lessons from leaders like the stories here, you already on the right track forward.

- The best ideas can come at any moment and entrepreneurs run toward challenges and pain points as business opportunities, while others see them as obstacles. Some innovations are driven by a solution-first approach that is looking for the right target market.

- The eureka moment and differentiation can come in many shapes: the idea itself, novel technology, marketing strategy, community it supports location, etc. The key is to align the company goals with the strategy you will use to get there.

- Startup ideas/eureka moments can come from personal challenges faced as well as business pain points. Be on the lookout for ways to tie these together in a unique solution. Market validation is key. Let the customers decide what is a good idea and what does not work.

- Feedback is king in shaping your startup and it's okay to do things early that do not scale. There are ways to test the waters and validate a concept before jumping all in with both feet and scaling for mass-market adoption. Find an eager customer early and work to solve their needs.

- Make yourself known to the people you want to connect with, read their books, attend their events, or host events of your own.

- Timing can be a blessing and a curse. Be nimble and adaptable while protecting your startup from risk where you can.
- Failure is expected but using other people's failures to breed success is ideal. Always expect the unexpected and be set up to adapt.
- Living a balanced lifestyle is key to avoiding burnout and keeping the same passion for your work that you start with on day one.
- Watch who uses your platform and how to focus on the most important features. Successful startups have simple concepts they execute well. It is okay to take a step back, a walk on the beach and think. Some of the best ideas come outside of the office.
- Bet on the jockey, not the horse. A great entrepreneur can find new directions and pivots for the company that may not have even been part of the original concept.
- View every encounter with investors as a chance to build relationships, even a pitch contest may turn into an opportunity much bigger than you expected. Not every investor is right for every company; do your diligence on them as well while they evaluate your company.
- The most important part of a pitch is the story you tell.

Now venture forward and let your startup story unfold.

ACKNOWLEDGEMENTS

I'd like to also thank everyone who pre-ordered my book. Your financial support made this book and it's publication possible. I'd like to take a moment to individually thank everyone who pre-ordered my book:

Nkosi Nurse
Michael Riemer
Florence Mugenyi
Ted Finn
David Gertler
Nuri Al-Hakim
Kevin Palmer
Marcy and Brian Kessler
Timothy Roe
Jeremy Fransman

Jeff Champagne

Anmol Wassan

Jean Hammond

Eric Gilliland

John Lohavichan

Michael Mullaley

Robert Costello

Eric Koester

Jim DiBona

Mic Williams

Jeremy Reich

Yevgeny Ioffe

Jake Schwartz

Clara Arroyave

Angelo Perrina

Janis and Rick Brodmerkle

Billmon Ng

Tony Martignetti

John Wood

Steven and Nancy Spirito

Donald Sandler

Melissa Lewin

Farhan Abassi

David J. Paliotti

Zwede Hewitt

Samon Saneback

Florence Furaha

Zack Rubinstein

Michael Hannon

Murtada Alnamer

Jonah Lupton

Erik Bullen

Karthik Kuppuswamy

Joshua Lustbader

Joe Wilson

Chris Lambert

Alland Timas

Brett Baron

James and Maryann DiBona

Nancy Shone

Sang Nam

Brett Andrews

I'd like to especially thank the people who invested more in my publishing and pre-ordered multiple copies of my book.

With special thanks to:

Andy, Robin and Adam Kraus

Helen, Mike and Nina Vlasic

Kelly and Walter Hinds

Holly and Greg Hines
Equity Venture Partners

Thank you to everyone. Your financial support allowed me to transform countless pages of notes and interviews into the book you are about to read.